nēhiyawētān kīkināhk

Speaking Cree in the Home

A Beginner's Guide for Families

Belinda Daniels & Andrea Custer

FOREWORD BY *Solomon Ratt*
ILLUSTRATIONS BY *Lana Whiskeyjack*

© 2022 Belinda Daniels and Andrea Custer

All rights reserved. No part of this work covered by the copyrights hereon may be reproduced or used in any form or by any means—graphic, electronic, or mechanical—without the prior written permission of the publisher. Any request for photocopying, recording, taping or placement in information storage and retrieval systems of any sort shall be directed in writing to Access Copyright.

COVER AND TEXT DESIGN: Duncan Noel Campbell
COPY EDITOR: Marionne Cronin
PROOFREADER: Donna Grant
COVER ART: detail of painting by Lana Whiskeyjack

Library and Archives Canada Cataloguing in Publication

TITLE: nēhiyawētān kīkināhk = Speaking Cree in the home : a beginner's guide for families / Belinda Daniels & Andrea Custer ; foreword by Solomon Ratt ; illustrations by Lana Whiskeyjack.

OTHER TITLES: Speaking Cree in the home

NAMES: Daniels, Belinda, author. | Custer, Andrea (Andrea Sherry), author. | Ratt, Solomon, writer of foreword. | Whiskeyjack, Lana, illustrator.

DESCRIPTION: Includes bibliographical references.

IDENTIFIERS: Canadiana (print) 20220391254 | Canadiana (ebook) 20220391440 | ISBN 9780889779037 (hardcover) | ISBN 9780889779006 (softcover) | ISBN 9780889779013 (PDF) | ISBN 9780889779020 (EPUB)

SUBJECTS: LCSH: Cree language—Study and teaching (Early childhood) | LCSH: Cree language—Self-instruction.

CLASSIFICATION: LCC PM986 .D36 2022 | DDC 497/.32380071—dc23

10 9 8 7 6 5 4 3 2 1

University of Regina Press

University of Regina, Regina, Saskatchewan, Canada, S4S 0A2
TEL: (306) 585-4758 FAX: (306) 585-4699
WEB: www.uofrpress.ca

We acknowledge the support of the Canada Council for the Arts for our publishing program. We acknowledge the financial support of the Government of Canada. / Nous reconnaissons l'appui financier du gouvernement du Canada. This publication was made possible with support from Creative Saskatchewan's Book Publishing Production Grant Program.

ōma masinahikan nēhiyaw awāsisak
anohc ēkwa ōtē nīkān ohci.

*This book is for the Cree children
of today and the future.*

Contents

Foreword by Solomon Ratt **xi**

Part One: nēhiyaw pīkiskwēwin ācimowin / *The History of the Cree Language*

nēhiyawak / *The nēhiyawak* **3**

kahkiyaw nanātohk nēhiyawak / *Locating the Many Different Types of Cree People* **9**

ohtaskānēsiwin ācimowina / *Stories of 'Place'* **13**

āhtaskēwi-mōskīstākēwin / *The Invasion* **17**

kayāsi-kiskinwahamākosiwin kiki kāwi ka-kī-ohpinikātēk pīkiskwēwin / *A Brief History of Indigenous Ways of Learning, with a Focus on Language Revitalization* **21**

iyiniw-ayisiyinīw kiskinawahamātowin / *Indigenous Education* **23**

ka-wanāhikoyahk nēhiyaw kiskinawahamātowin / *The Interruption of nēhiyaw Lifelong Learning* **25**

kāwī-kimiskāsonaw—iyiniw-ayisiyinīwiwin pimātisiwin ē-ohpinamahk / *Finding Our Way Back—Indigenous Reclamation* **27** iyiniw-ayisiyinīwiwin pīkiskwēwin ka-ohpinamahk—at(i)-nīkān / *Indigenous Language Reclamation—The Way Forward* 31

Part Two: kā–āsōnamākēhk / *Leaving a Legacy*

Hay little rez girl, what is your destiny? 35

kā-sākōcihikoyahk ēkwa kā-ātawēyihtamahk mōniyāw māmitonēyihcikan / *Colonization and Decolonization* 37

ohtaskānēsiwin ēkwa pimohtēhiwin / *Roots and Routes* 39

pīkikiskwēwin ēkwa nēhiyawātisiwin ispīhtēyihtākwan / *The Value of Language and Way of Being* 43

ēwako kā-sākihitāyan, kimiyikosiwin anima / *Your Passion Is Your Gift* 47

miyo-ohpikihāwasowin / *Good Child-Rearing* 49

Part Three: sōskwāc ta–āpacihtāyēk nēhiyawēwin kīkiwāhk / *The Practical Application of Cree in the Home*

CHAPTER ONE: okāwīmāw ōma niya / *I Am a Mother* 55

CHAPTER TWO: mācihtātān / *Let's Begin* 59

CHAPTER THREE: osihtā pīkiskwēwin kaskihtāwina / *Setting Language Goals* **67**

CHAPTER FOUR: kā-miyo-āpatahki kīkwaya / *Methods* **71**

CHAPTER FIVE: āpacihcikana / *Resources* **77**

CHAPTER SIX: ka-ayamihtāhk nēhiyawasinahikēwin / *Reading Cree Standard Roman Orthography* **83**

CHAPTER SEVEN: ka-nēhiyawēyan kīkihk / *Speaking Cree Around the Home* **91**

CHAPTER EIGHT: nēhiyawēwin itwēwina / *Cree Vocabulary* **93**

CHAPTER NINE: mitātahtomitanaw māwaci kā-āpatahki itwēwina / *100 High-Frequency Words and Phrases* **107**

CHAPTER TEN: isīhcikēwina kiya ēkwa kicawāsimis ohci / *Activities for You and Your Child* **115**

CHAPTER ELEVEN: sīhkimitowina / *Inspirational Quotes* **157**

nanāskomowin / *Acknowledgements* **163**

Notes **167**
References **169**

Foreword

This is a welcome book for all who are interested in learning the Cree language, either for themselves alone or for themselves and their families. The book offers good guidance on the best practices in language learning based on the authors' personal experiences in their respective language journeys. Cree is a second language for Belinda, while it is Andrea's first language. Having a second-language learner and a first-language speaker collaborate on a book about learning a language is helpful because a lot of the time the first-language learner has no idea what works for the second-language learner. Often the first-language speaker tends to take the value of her/his language for granted and to assume that what was easy for him/her in learning the language ought to come easy for the second-language learner. This, of course, is not the case. First-language speakers teaching the language to second-language learners must at all times be patient with the language learner. Perhaps this is the most important thing to remember about language teaching and language learning: as an instructor, be patient with your students; as a learner, be patient with yourself.

Belinda and Andrea start the book with a brief history of language revitalization efforts in Canada and elsewhere. They then offer their own linguistic autobiographies, which give us insights into both language learning and language teaching. Belinda started learning Cree at the University of Saskatchewan, and Andrea is a fluent speaker who started teaching Cree after taking a class at the University of Alberta where she came to see the value of her language. Belinda started to coordinate language experience summer camps as part of her learning experience. Andrea joined one of the camps a few years later, and together they have been working to find the best methods for learning and teaching the Cree language. The language experience camps are popular, and in recent years the nēhiyaw language experience group has offered weekend sessions in both Saskatoon and Regina for interested people who want to learn the Cree language. Both Belinda and Andrea know that the best way to learn a language is through immersion. The situation in most urban settings, however, does not allow the conditions for immersion because, once the students leave the classroom, they go back to a predominately English-speaking milieu. This book offers ways in which these students can pursue their studies—on their own or with their families—based on the experiences from both Belinda and Andrea.

Belinda and Andrea, kinanāskomitināwāw (*I thank you both*)for writing this book. I know it will be a helpful resource, a much-needed resource at that. āhkamēyimok!

Solomon Ratt
Associate Professor of Cree Language Studies
First Nations University of Canada

PART ONE

nēhiyaw pīkiskwēwin ācimowin

The History of the Cree Language

nēhiyawak

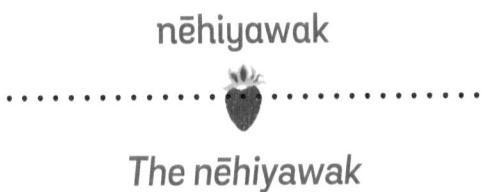

The nēhiyawak

The nēhiyawak (*the Plains Cree people*) were one of the Indigenous populations living in what is now Saskatchewan. They lived in the parklands areas and on the prairies of what is now known as Saskatchewan and Alberta. They traded and forged partnerships and alliances with many of their neighbours. Cree people say that they have always been here. The Cree have many of the place names still noted in language, like that of Saskatchewan: kisiskāciwan in Cree.

According to the teachings of the 'Old Ones' like Barry Ahenakew, Keith Goulet, and the late Simon Kyhtwethat, we have stories from even before the great flood (the biblical myth of Noah's Ark), known as sacred ātayōhkēwina stories. However, the story of the creation of these lands comes from wīsahkēcāhk after the great flood. It was with the help of Otter, Beaver, and Muskrat that wīsahkēcāhk helped create this new island, sometimes referred to as Turtle Island, that we inhabit today. wīsahkēcāhk had helped make this island and created our people here, our ancestors. It should be noted that stories are methods of transmitting history, culture, and teachings, and are metaphors for practical application today, as they provide instructions for wāhkōhtowin (*kinship*) and miyo-pimātisiwin (*a good life*).

There are many versions of this story told across Algonquian Nations. Ella Elizabeth Clark's *Indian Legends of Canada* contains one example, which is said to have been told to and recorded by David Thompson before the arrival of the missionaries.[1] Clark's retelling of the story begins this way:

> After Creator had made all the animals and had made the first people, he said to Wisakedjak, "Take good care of my people, and teach them how to live. Show them all the bad roots, all the roots that will hurt them and kill them. Do not let the people or the animals quarrel with each other."
>
> But Wisakedjak did not obey the Creator. He let the creatures do whatever they wished to do. Soon they were quarrelling and fighting and shedding much blood.

As the story continues, we find out that the Creator was very unhappy with Wisakedjak and warned him that continued disobedience would have dire consequences. But Wisakedjak did not change his ways; in fact, his behaviour worsened:

> Becoming more and more careless and disobedient, [Wisakedjak] tricked the animals and the people and made them angry with each other. They quarrelled and fought so much that the earth became red with blood.
> This time the Creator became very angry. "I will take everything away from you and wash the ground clean," he said.
> Still Wisakedjak did not believe the Creator. He did not believe until the rains came and the streams began to swell. Day after day, and night after night, the rains continued. The water in the rivers and the lakes rose higher and higher. At last they overflowed their banks and washed the ground clean. The sea came up on the land, and everything was drowned except one Otter, one Beaver, and one Muskrat.
> Wisakedjak tried to stop the sea, but it was too strong for him. He sat down on the water and wept. Otter, Beaver, and Muskrat sat beside him and rested their heads on one of his thighs.

At last the rain stopped, the story tells us, and the Creator took pity on Wisakedjak. The Creator granted him the power to remake the world—but only by using the original materials that were now under the sea.

Wisakedjak turned to his companions—Otter, Beaver, and Muskrat—and implored each in turn to dive into the sea and retrieve a bit of the old earth, which was now deep under the water. In return, he promised them food, shelter, and a wife. Otter and Beaver tried—three times each—but came up empty. Beaver was nearly dead when he returned from his third dive.

Now only Muskrat was left. He dived twice, with no success, except that when he returned the second time, Wisakedjak detected the smell of earth on his paws. He sent Muskrat back down into the water for a third time:

> This time Muskrat stayed so long that Wisakedjak feared he had drowned. At last they saw some bubbles coming up through the water. Wisakedjak reached down his long arm, seized Muskrat and pulled him up beside them. The little creature was almost dead, but against his breast his forepaws held a piece of the old earth.
>
> Joyously, Wisakedjak seized it, and in a short time he had expanded the bit of earth into an island. There he, Muskrat, Otter, and Beaver rested and rejoiced that they had not drowned in the flood.
>
> Some people say that Wisakedjak obtained a bit of wood, from which he made the trees; that he obtained some bones, from which he made the second race of animals.
>
> Others say that the Creator made all things again. He commanded the rivers to take the salt

water back to the sea. Then he created mankind, the animals of today, and the trees. He took from Wisakedjak all power over people and animals and left him only the power to flatter and to deceive.

After that, Wisakedjak played tricks upon the animals and led them into much mischief. That is why the Indians tell many stories about him, to amuse themselves during the long winter evenings.

This is where time and creation started for this world we live in now; however, Cree people know time goes back much further than that.

Settler historian Bill Waiser writes about a veteran of the fur trade from 1823 whose name was George Nelson and who worked for the Hudson Bay Company in La Ronge, Saskatchewan.[2] Nelson also recorded a version of the story which tells of the making of the world after the great flood; however, what is unique in his story was that the making of people resulted because wīsahkēcāhk grew lonely. Waiser quotes this excerpt from Nelson's journal:

> Now after some time [wīsahkēcāhk] became very lonesome and bethought himself of making Indians [We don't like this word and do not promote using it], i.e., human beings. He in consequence took up a stone and fashioned it into the form of a man; but whilst at this work it struck him that by forming them of so strong

and hard a substance that in time when they would come to know their nature, they would grow insolent and rebellious and be a great annoyance to each other and of course also would never die. "This will not do, I must make them of a more weak and fragile substance, so that they may live a reasonable time and behave as becomes human beings." Upon this he took up a handful of common Earth and made a form of a man and blew into his nostrils the breath of life.[3]

Nelson's journal expressed a belief that Cree people were made here, that they are made from the very soil of Turtle Island. We believe this, like so many other Cree people believe this. Many of our stories, our oral histories, our songs are imprinted on these lands. Both nēhiyawak and settler historians can agree on this fact.

kahkiyaw nanātohk nēhiyawak

Locating the Many Different Types of Cree People

At one time, collectively we, the Plains Cree from the Sturgeon Lake, SK, area, were once known as the pēhocīn nēhiyawak and before that the pīkokimāw nēhiyawak. Our names relate to the lands which our ancestors occupied.

The nēhiyawak—also known as the 'Cree' people, as previously mentioned—(we) are the largest Nation within what we now call Canada. Cree speakers live right across Canada, from British Columbia through Quebec, and into the United States. Hints of our histories of migration, although hidden in the landscape of the land, can still be seen and are told in place-based stories to this day.

Our ancestors and their names can be found in the lands, the lakes and rivers, and the places we once inhabited and can now be read in documented history books. Early records written by explorers like La Vérendrye, Hudson Bay Company employees like Henry Kelsey and Anthony Henday, and other fur traders like Alexander Henry document how they interacted and sometimes lived with the Cree people. It is known that early settlers learned our Indigenous languages. A couple hundred years later, in the early to mid-1900s, anthropologist David Mandelbaum also lived with the Cree, documenting their livelihoods, leaving us evidence of what Cree people have always said about their lives and culture.

Due to early Europeans coming to settle here, diseases like smallpox were brought over, tragically killing huge populations of these Cree groups. As previously mentioned, one of the many Cree groups known were the Pegogamaw Cree, which meant rough, jagged, rocky shores all along the North Saskatchewan River. The Cree word pīkokamāw literally means 'broken body of water' and refers to the broken shoreline of the Saskatchewan River.

The Woodland Cree territory was in the northern regions, along the large waterways of misinipiy (*the Churchill River*): misi- meaning 'large,' nipiy meaning 'water.' The Swampy Cree people lived in the mid-central area of what is now Saskatchewan and into what is now Manitoba. The Cree term Basquia (opāskēyāk—The Pas) refers to the location of the Saskatchewan River Delta; Basquia is actually spelled paskwāyāw, meaning 'big meadow,' or paskwāw, meaning a clearing or prairie. These are examples of how the names of these Cree people tell us something about where they lived on the land.

Cree people and their complex system of language can now be categorized into five dialects that differ by the sounds

Cree people use: Plains Cree (the 'Y' dialect), Swampy Cree (the 'N' dialect), Moose Cree (the 'L' dialect), Woods Cree (the 'TH' dialect), and East Cree (the 'R' dialect). The Plains Cree speak using a 'Y' dialect and live on the prairies and areas to the northwest. The 'TH' dialect speakers are referred to as the Woods Cree, who also refer to themselves as the 'Rock Cree.' They lived to the north, past the prairie regions. The Swampy Cree live in the mid-central area of Saskatchewan (Cumberland House) and into northern Manitoba and Ontario. Farther east in Canada, in and around the Hudson Bay area, the dialect spoken is the 'L' dialect. Lastly, the 'R' dialect represents the Quebec area, sometimes known as the dialect of the Atikamek Cree.

These dialects changed according to the environment. There are noted differences with the dialects across Canada. The 'Y' and 'TH' dialects, for instance, can understand one another but do have vocabulary differences. These two groups have been living and trading in the same area for a long time. Because their sounds are a little different, most Cree-speaking people can determine where a person is from by the dialect they speak. However, the Cree people who speak Moose or Atikamek Cree sound very different from the 'Y' and 'TH' speakers and are not readily understandable to the Western Cree.

After the immigration of the Europeans and land loss for Indigenous peoples in the late 1880s, rapid changes occurred due to the decline of great herds of bison, the fur trading system putting pressure on the reproduction and growth of many fur-bearing animals such as the beaver, the people's vulnerability to diseases, and then the treaty making process, which then resulted in the reservation system.

The reserve system is not a normal occurrence. The result of treaty signing and the *Indian Act* of 1876, reserves were man-made and devised by the developing Canadian government. Despite these tragic changes though, what occurred on and with the land, the language and its relationship to places never stopped. The value of the land has always been in the heart and spirit of the nēhiyawak. We are still here, owning our heritage and practising our customs and sharing tradition with our families. nēhiyawak people speaking nēhiyawēwin shatters colonization.

ohtaskānēsiwin ācimowina

Stories of 'Place'

Belinda's ōhkoma (*grandmother*) says that people did not stay in a specific area for the whole year—meaning that, although she was raised in a log cabin, Cree people often travelled all over the place to hunt, trade, gather, visit, and most importantly, because of the need to feed themselves. When reminiscing about the old days, Belinda's ōhkoma can recall in her language some of the lakes and hills of the area she grew up in—places where she camped and lived, like Waskesiu in the Prince Albert National Park area. This is where her parents recalled hunting and fishing. Belinda's ōhkoma remembers these stories from when she was a child. She said that there was a lake known as kinosēw sākahikan (*Fish Lake* or *Fishing Lake*), which is near the Tweedsmuir area of Saskatchewan. Back in the day, when she was young, she said she remembers being able to drink water right out of the lake with her hands or with a bucket. The water had been so clean and fresh!

When Belinda was a child, she was often taken swimming in those same exact locations that her ōhkoma pointed out; these are places she swam as a child, and now Belinda's children go swimming there. Belinda learned a lot from her grandparents and the locations they knew well and now has passed on this information to her children. These are stories about 'place.'

For instance, Montreal Lake was known to Belinda's ōhkoma as mōniyāsis sākahikan, a location in Northern Saskatchewan, and wāwāskīsiw, as previously mentioned, was another location not far from Montreal Lake. This was known as the place of elk; it was also an important gathering place. It has been said by Belinda's relatives that people would carve out faces or silhouettes of people in the trees of this beautiful place to signify it was a communal spot. Belinda's ōhkoma also recalls that the city of Prince Albert was known as kistapinānihk because it is a big hill and, more significantly, was noted as a meeting place. This area was also known as a Sun Dance site to many other Nations in the area. These are more stories about 'place,' and our nēhiyaw identities are attached to these places.

The importance of Cree place names stays preserved as time goes on, remaining a part of the Cree collective memory to be passed on. The eventual process that occurred was that of changing Cree names to English ones. This was not only about diminishing identity but also about erasing the Cree names of places and disconnecting Cree people from their lands, and thus from their identity. The impact of such erasure was to hide people's ties to families' gathering places, to make people forget the stories, spaces, and places of significant happenings. This inheritance was deliberately stolen, banned, and outlawed by the colonial presence. In reclaiming language, we are reclaiming ties to the land and the sacred names of places. It is the land that gives us a sense of home, and language is attached to our identity.

nēhiyawak ōma kiyānaw, we are the Exact Body of People, our history is extensive, anything but easy. We are multi-faceted. Our identities are attached and expressed through songs, stories, prayers, and ceremonies. These expressions and intentions and memories are within the land itself, deep in the soil of the hills and meadows, seeped in the lakes and river systems. Most importantly, we are still here, like the land, and a part of these lands.

āhtaskēwi-mōskīstākēwin

The Invasion

It was around the late 1600s that the first European explorers arrived and came into the territory of what is now called Saskatchewan. The Hudson's Bay Company was created in 1670, and by this time a good relationship had developed between English Hudson's Bay Company traders and the Cree. Trade among the Europeans and the Cree brought many changes, and the English were often cautious when it came to the French, because the Hudson's Bay Company was also in the pursuit of the acquisition of land. Competition for territory between French and English traders became the prime nature of business between the early Europeans on Turtle Island.

Along with trade came a variety of diseases, which had hugely negative impacts on the Plains Indigenous Peoples, including the Cree. Trading alliances were formed, including peace and friendship treaties, which then turned into land transfers. In 1763 the Royal Proclamation was created, a proclamation created by the British to ensure peace between the settlers and Indigenous peoples and which acknowledged Indigenous lands. These treaties and the administrating of them created a different relationship between the Cree and the early Europeans. Priorities changed for the British and its government system. The smallpox epidemics also took their toll, weakening Indigenous Nations. The English and the French were quickly moving west onto the Plains. The Cree people population began to decline, along with their power and presence on the land.

In 1821, a huge merger took place between the Hudson's Bay Company and the North West Company, a competing fur trading company, and the fur trade began to decrease. Bison by this time had become nearly depleted. In the 1870s starvation swept among the Cree. The North-West Mounted Police (NWMP) began to appear in the west in 1874. The NWMP was created to ensure settlement in the west and not for any other purpose.

In Saskatchewan, Europans began to arrive and set up farms in the 1800s. The population of western Canada began to grow. The numbered post-Confederation treaties with Indigenous Peoples were signed between 1871 and 1921. Many Indigenous Nations start moving to and staying on reserves set aside for them. The Canadian Pacific Railway made its way across the country and was eventually completed. The *Dominion Lands Act* of 1872 was created, encouraging settlement by Europeans. The Canadian government also gave out 'free and promised' land to urge more European immigrants to move onto the Prairies to stay.

Government policies impacted Indigenous lives negatively, and these policies were in favour of the livelihood of European farmers. There was an enforced use of English in residential schools for Indigenous children. First Nations languages like Cree began to decline. The history of enforced schooling, its legacy, and "federal government involvement in Residential school did not begin in earnest until the 1880s . . . after the Canadian state was established in 1867."[4] This is the history of the nēhiyawak: the coming of 'schooling' assisted in the decline of and negative attitude toward our language. In many ways, residential schools broke down families and continued to shame people for speaking nēhiyawēwin. This affected many families and the intergenerational process of knowledge and language. Lack of self-worth and pride in Indigenous identity was a product of colonization and was an assimilation tactic.

kayāsi-kiskinwahamākosiwin kiki kāwi ka-kī-ohpinikātēk pīkiskwēwin

A Brief History of Indigenous Ways of Learning, with a Focus on Language Revitalization

nēhiyawātisiwin / Cree Life

This section discusses the various ideas of what nēhiyawātisiwin, or the Cree way of knowing and being, means from different perspectives. Prior to contact over 500 years ago, the Indigenous people of this continent thrived; they were able to meet all their needs through relationship with the land and its animals as these provided all the food, shelter, medicines, tools, and clothing that they needed. Later the Europeans arrived, hungry to settle on and exploit new lands. They not only intended to settle and exploit but they wanted to 'colonize' or replace Indigenous world view and languages with their own through forced assimilation by using Western education and religion.

Children were taken from their homes, from their traditional lands, to attend residential schools, often far away. Children suffered and endured physical, mental, sexual, and psychological abuse. The impacts of attending these schools would resonate far into the future.

Many years later, Indigenous people are on a path of reclaiming what was stolen and beaten out of them: their identity, language, and lands. Although education was the tool that was used to destroy Indigenous lives, education is now being used again, this time for the purpose of restoring and reclaiming nēhiyawātisiwin.

iyiniw-ayisiyinīw kiskinawahamātowin

Indigenous Education

The way Indigenous people learn and understand this world is very different from how Europeans learn and understand this world. There are many brilliant Indigenous scholars such as Leroy Little Bear, Marie Battiste, Gregory Cajete, and Willie Ermine, to name a few, who have researched Indigenous ways of learning; they have revealed that Indigenous learning is wholistic, and other interactions included are: listening, silence, relationships, cycles, stillness, spirituality, and an understanding of the notion of place, time, and space, as well as individuals' roles and responsibilities to the world around them. For instance, listening means being able to understand lessons as they are being told in the oral tradition, such as storytelling—the story itself takes the listener beyond time and space. Silence is another way of learning and is a place of inspiration and finding answers. Silence is comforting for us, as Indigenous people, and helps us stay present, but may be uncomfortable for non-Indigenous people. Relationships are another pivotal teaching; relationships are the key to everything, seen and unseen—this is about responsibility and accountability to our families and communities. Cycles are about a way of life, a process, a way of being; they are about accepting the 'flow' and 'changes' when journeying through life, and not trying to control what cannot be controlled. Time and space, these are about ceremonies and celebrations. For example, annual Sun Dances, or powwows, or even language camps can only be celebrated by being present and taking action for these specific purposes during certain times of the year. They just happen, as they are to happen.

The way we learn still exists within us; although it may have been interrupted, it has not been forgotten or destroyed. It is embedded into our unconscious, languages, and world view. With the help of 'Old Ones' and their knowledge, Indigenous people are on a path of restoring and reclaiming Indigenous ways of knowing and being, including languages, traditions, and teachings.

ka-wanāhikoyahk nēhiyaw kiskinawahamātowin

The Interruption of nēhiyaw Lifelong Learning

In the 1940s and 1950s, after World War II, there came a shift of policies and education moved towards becoming more inclusive for Indigenous people. This was due to the pressure of Indigenous leaders, such as Joseph Dreaver, who wanted education that did not intend to assimilate Indigenous people into mainstream Canada.

At the time, there was a push for proper education and languages were not yet an issue. It was still spoken, but not as rigorously as it once had. The use of the Cree language had begun to lose its hold on the younger generations; a language shift was evident as English was preferred over Cree for multiple reasons. Rejection of language was rooted in the 'schooling' at residential schools, the *Indian Act,* and the continued pressure to assimilate.

In the community of Sturgeon Lake, Saskatchewan, people born before the 1960s were fluent in Cree. People born after this saw the language transmission from parents and grandparents to children interrupted and children began to cease speaking Cree.

kāwī-kimiskāsonaw—
iyiniw-ayisiyinīwiwin
pimātisiwin ē-ohpinamahk

Finding Our Way Back—
Indigenous Reclamation

In the 1970s racism was rampant in provincial schools and so Indigenous leaders began to push for "Indian Control of Indian Education." Education was to be controlled by the bands. There was little support from government, but Indigenous people still found a way to deliver the education they wanted for their children in churches, homes, and community halls until they had their own schools.

Around 1972, a Cree ad hoc committee from the Saskatchewan Indian Cultural Centre met to discuss how Cree language programming should be delivered. Immersion programming, it seemed, would be an ideal way of delivering Cree language programming. However, some communities resisted because their children were still speaking Cree, and English was a priority. Other communities, though, had a strong desire for a Cree language program. It was noted in their meeting notes that language use was still declining.

In the 1980s language revitalization began, with Hawai'i and New Zealand blazing trails for the rest of their Indigenous brothers and sisters to follow, although it is important to note that French immersion has been in existence in Canada for a long time—the Maori and the Hawaiians came to Canada to see French immersion in action. Having faced similar struggles, they understood that language reclamation and transmission is key in self-determination and sovereignty. They have been highly successful in developing language nests and immersion programs in their elementary, secondary, and university programs. In both Hawai'i and New Zealand, their Indigenous languages are now considered official languages by law.

The Mohawk in Canada were the first to start immersion in their Kaien'keha program in Kahnawake, Quebec. This started in 1979, and is now the longest running Indigenous language program in Canada. They have had many trials and tribulations when it comes to maintaining funds and community support. But most importantly, they have been successful in creating Mohawk speakers!

Back in Saskatchewan, the Denesuline opened the Clearwater River Dene School in 2007. "A strong foundation in the first language ... was seen as a precondition to successful second language ... learning."[5] The school is from Headstart level (preschool) to grade four. The community wants children to be successful in bilingualism and to have a strong Dene identity. Successful assessment practices included reading levels on par with the rest of the province in 2011.[6] Parental involvement is significant because of the commonality of language. One challenge is that there is no writing system, which is time consuming when it comes to creating and localizing curriculum and implementation. Other challenges include a lack of resources designed for the grades at hand. Despite these challenges, the school continues to grow and troubleshoot in bilingualism.

In retrospect, it is interesting to point out that the last residential school in Canada closed in 1996. Some band-controlled schools now have begun their process of language revitalization, a handful of schools are successfully delivering Indigenous language programming, and more schools are beginning to seriously consider how to best deliver a language program as awareness about the value of Indigenous languages continue to grow. We have given only a small sample of these.

iyiniw-ayisiyinīwiwin pīkiskwēwin ka-ohpinamahk—at(i)-nīkān

Indigenous Language Reclamation— The Way Forward

In 2015 the Truth and Reconciliation Commission Report provided five Calls to Action specifically for language and cultural revitalization. In June of 2019, the *Indigenous Language Act* was passed in Canada. This Act claimed to help and support Indigenous languages, but what is interesting to note is that this came with no financial support or guidance from the Canadian government. Other significant issues confronting efforts to revitalize Indigenous languages are the lack of resources, curriculum created from Indigenous perspectives, and monies, and a lack of fluent speakers highly trained in language development, language teaching practices and second-language acquisition theories.

We also need to be dedicated, passionate, and courageous because language work is challenging but fulfilling work.

Presently, language teachers are overworked and underappreciated in some communities and mainstream schools. This reflects the attitudes towards the Cree language and its value. English as a second language for immigrants and other core subjects are considered a higher priority within mainstream education, while the Cree language has a lesser status.

There is also the issue of where language teachers can go to get the best kind of training or what that training looks like. Places such as the Canadian Indigenous Languages and Literacy Development Institute (CILLDI) housed at the University of Alberta, Blue Quills College, First Nations University of Canada, and the University of Victoria offer these courses, but as yet there seems to be no unified vision of how to best deliver language programming that leads to fluency.

What is most clear is that in order to successfully reclaim and revitalize Indigenous languages there are several things that need to occur. The most important thing is to raise awareness of the Cree language. The value of knowing a second language, in this case Cree, to both Indigenous people and the rest of Canadian society is a benefit to all of us. We need this understood in order to acquire and pressure the government for both financial and community support.

Nations, communities, grassroots organizations—top-down, bottom-up—families, and individuals themselves need to be invested in their own language reclamation journey. Most importantly, parents with children in language programming are key in the continuity of efforts because the language must be heard outside of school and be valued in the home.

PART TWO

kā-āsōnamākēhk

Leaving a Legacy

Hay little rez girl, what is your destiny?

Little rez girl from the bush & the bronx
raised Catholic
provincially programmed
university educated
teacher
my fate was supposed to be assimilashun; to write & talk englis,
to dream about & value
those european concepts and things above family & community
... power, money, fast boats, fancy
trucks, expensive clothes, lavish vacays, god, resource extraction & status
but
trailblazers intervened
and the ancestors had other plans
instead i fell in love with my brown skin, hair & eyes,
realized that nīhithaw land,
language & identity is the antidote to the sickness of colonization &
capitalism
in my dna
the ancestors left for me
dreams & visions for something better than this nightmare we find
ourselves in
the understandings of what nīhithaw pimātisiwin is
how dignity is our birthright if we want it back
nīhithowīwin ka-wīhtamākon tānisi ta-isi-pimohtatāyān kipimātisiwin

ikwa
ka-kiskisīyan kihci-kiskinwāhamākīwina
The Cree language will show you how to live your life
and
remember the teachings

Written in the 'TH' Cree dialect by Andrea Custer

kā–sākōcihikoyahk ēkwa kā–ātawēyihtamahk mōniyāw māmitonēyihcikan

Colonization and Decolonization

It should be noted that much of what I (Andrea) write is from my perspective as an asinīskāwiskwīw, a Rock Cree woman, from the reserve of Pelican Narrows or wapāwikoscikanihk, which means Narrows of Fear, and from the traditional lands and territories of my grandparents, great-grandparents, and ancestors known in English as Uskik (askihk) Lake and Iskwatam Lake. I am also an aspiring Indigenous scholar and mother of five children. Like many Indigenous people, I have faced many hardships and traumas brought on by government policies such as residential schools and the *Indian Act*. There are many stories such as mine, because the traumas we have faced and continue to face as Indigenous people are everywhere.

It is the year 2022 and we are living in an interesting era. Recently there have been a string of events, such as the

Wet'suwet'en opposition to having a pipeline built right through their traditional territories and the Colten Boushie case, where a young Indigenous man was murdered for allegedly 'trespassing.' In 2012, there were Idle No More protests that sparked an awakening of our inherent rights but also our responsibilities to the lands and identities as Indigenous people. Before this, we had the Oka Crisis in 1990, which was a land dispute between the Mohawk and the provincial government of Quebec. These are a few of the significant events that happened for Indigenous people around the world. Before they happened, Indigenous people were not aware of the impact colonialism had on Indigenous lives, families, and communities and how it has harmfully affected our minds, attitudes, emotions, and spirits.

The term colonialism describes how the government has tried to take and continues to try taking over lands and traditional systems by settling on our lands, creating reserves, and establishing residential schools, through provincial schools, day schools, the '60s Scoop, and the media. The government has many tools in its belt to achieve their goals. Assimilation describes getting rid of Indigenous languages and world views and replacing them with the English language and the European world view—all go hand in hand with colonialism. Always, the goal is to have us forget our own languages, values, beliefs, treaties, and our ties to our lands. Decolonization, then, is the word for peeling away those European values and beliefs that are not Indigenous and setting out to take back our rights to our own languages, systems, values, beliefs, practices, and rights to our lands. It is a journey that is both healing and empowering.

ohtaskānēsiwin ēkwa pimohtēhiwin

Roots and Routes

As I return to memories of my roots, I understand that my childhood was full of love, but it was also unhealthy due to the traumas brought on by government assimilation policies. I had the opportunity to experience life on our traditional lands at Uskik (askihk) Lake and Iskwatam Lake along the māhtāwisīpiy (*the Churchill River*) in northern Saskatchewan with family, language, and ancestral teachings of living on the land in a respectful manner. I swam in the lakes and ran in the bushes with reckless freedom along with my sisters and brothers, who were my first best friends. We were always taught to be mindful of our behaviour; at an early age we learned about pāstāhowin,[7] pāstāmowin,[8] and ohcinēwin[9]: our Natural and sacred laws which gave us the morals and values to abide by, given to us by kisē-manitow (*kind, compassionate, and loving Creator*) and passed down through the generations. At that time I never really thought about these as teachings because they were a part of who we were. My family gave me everything that I needed to remember to be proud of who I am: language, kinship, teachings, and love for the land. Those early memories of my childhood are the ones I cherish the most; they are also what would lead me to my life's purpose as an asinīskāwiskwēw (*Rock Cree woman*).

On the other hand, because of residential schools I grew up in Pelican Narrows living in a wounded world. My grandparents, parents, and I all attended residential schools. The biggest impact of the traumas that residential schools caused came from my maternal grandparents. Their ability to parent with love and good child-rearing teachings were impacted, to what extent I am not exactly sure. My maternal grandmother's mother (my great-grandmother) had passed away when she was very young and my late grandmother was sent to residential school, where she experienced abuses of all sorts, as did my late grandfather. It is not difficult to imagine now why it was so difficult for her to show any affection towards her children, because very little, if any, had been shown to her. Hugging and telling someone you love them was challenging for her. Before she passed, she was able to say, "I love you," and hug people, which spoke volumes of her own healing journey. My maternal grandfather, on the other hand, had alcohol addiction issues. I am eternally grateful that I did not see that side of him. I always remember him as the man who taught me about love and kindness and my grandmother as the person who taught me about strength and faith. One day, my late grandmother (paternal) Maggie walked out in the middle of a fierce storm and a tree landed on the tent she had just walked into. We were so scared for her as we cried, and all of a sudden she walked out of the tent and then came back into the cabin and said to us kids, "kāwitha wīhkāc kīkway kostamok."[10] That was her way of teaching us to be courageous and to have faith.

I was raised by a single mother who was a hard-working lone parent who also had experienced intergenerational trauma, and so I experienced intergenerational trauma as well. Still, she taught me about my identity, language, independence, and perseverance. My mother passed on the ethic of hard work to me; I will always honour her for that. My late father was not a huge presence in my life as I grew up, but I will always remember my time spent with him and my paternal grandmother at Iskwatam Lake. As I got older, I would spend more time with my late father, and he would often share his stories about othāpahcikīw[11] and his powers. He imparted a gift of knowledge and interest about my own history.

Other early memories are of going to a Roman Catholic church, learning about God, kneeling, repenting, and sinning. I remember always being fearful and felt shame early on. In school I learned how to read and write in English while learning about the history of Canada, but I don't remember learning a lot about my own Indigenous history, residential schools, or my own spiritual culture. I was fortunate that I was a curious little girl.

I remember as a young child looking at people abusing alcohol or getting high and thinking, why is my world like this? But I was also curious about who my people were. One day I picked up a book about vision quests and I felt so fascinated. That book opened a whole new world for me. I began to write about my dreams and interpreted them myself because there were no Elders that I knew of to turn to about these things. Maybe my grandparents, but I had never heard them talk about such things.

In any case, that curious and critical nature shaped my path in life. Later, I would learn about the 'dominant syntax' of English and education so that I could use it to understand power and oppression in order to articulate my Indigenous female voice in my life's work: serving people by helping revitalize language and culture while addressing colonial structures.

pīkikiskwēwin ēkwa nēhiyawātisiwin ispīhtēyihtākwan

The Value of Language and Way of Being

Over at the University of Alberta in 2012, I minored in teaching a second language for Cree. A good friend had suggested that I switch my minor because I was a fluent speaker and Cree teachers would be in demand. I had no idea! I was naïve to the power that I carried in my Cree fluency. As a matter of fact, I did not think it was anything special or important. This attitude is reflected in my own failure to pass on the language to my older children.

In that program I had the opportunity to understand that Cree language and culture was at risk. I felt shocked. One day as I sat in that class, I looked around and realized that I was the only Indigenous woman there. There were language teachers for French, Spanish, German, Mandarin, and Arabic, but I was the only one for Cree. It occurred to me at that moment exactly how vulnerable our Cree languages were. For any one of those other languages, you can go to those countries and be immersed in them, but here we only had ourselves and our communities.

Sometimes I am filled with doubt about the challenge of revitalizing language, because at times it seems like an uphill battle! One day I was feeling discouraged and so I asked an Elder about why we need to continue passing on our language and he said to me, "What are we fighting for?" I pondered about that question for a long time and realized that our language is tied to who we are as Cree people. Language is tied to our culture, beliefs, the lands, and, finally, it is tied to our sovereignty. It is everything that we need to resist assimilation. Embedded in our languages are our beliefs about how we are to carry ourselves in this world and how we are to treat others. I feel a huge sense of pride when I study our Cree language. For example, the word "kisē-manitow" refers to our Creator, who is implied to be kind, compassionate, and loving all in one word.

Other words in Cree related to the root word of "kisē-" are "kisē-ayak," which refers to the plural form of elderly people. It is presumed that they are to be kind, compassionate, and loving elders. kisēwātisiwin means kindness in Cree and it's one of the values that we as Cree people aspire to live by. Many times, as I was growing up, I would hear my family members say "kisēwātisi" or "be kind"; I learned later that it is related to our Natural law of kindness and it is an attribute of a good person. I am always astonished when I see the intricate connections between Cree words, beliefs, attitudes, and actions—they are incredibly beautiful.

Cree is the language of our ancestors. It is ancient and it has survived this long, through generations, despite the efforts to pluck it from our minds, hearts, and spirits. Rooted in our languages are the ideas, values, beliefs, and experiences of our ancestors. Language is beneficial; when a people can speak their language, it is said to have a direct impact on their mental health. It provides a sense of positive self-identity, pride, and increased self-esteem, and a bonus is that it makes you smarter.

Language is the building block of community; language is the glue that builds and holds a community together. When a community shares a language there is a sense of belonging, comfort, and solidarity, more so when the community has hung on to the teachings embedded in the language. Without it, we feel a sense of disconnection. Language is the building block of Nationhood when we speak a common language.

There are traditional government, leadership, kinship, and Natural law terms that provide instructions on how a community is to carry out its roles and responsibilities. These are beautiful and powerful. I also strongly believe that language can be good economically, as interest in local Indigenous communities is growing. People want to see and experience the world through our understandings; this is most possible through the language because of the world view that is embedded within it.

Now and in the future, travel to experience authentic Indigenous experiences will become more in demand. This provides an opportunity for local Indigenous communities to regain a sense of pride in their culture and in their language; they all have some beautiful gift to offer to the world. Our ancestors fought for this and I am positive that they would be filled with happiness, peace, and pride.

ēwako kā-sākihitāyan, kimiyikosiwin anima

.... 🍓 ....

Your Passion Is Your Gift

We were all born with gifts; we have them because Creator gave them to us and, whatever gift that was, it would lead to our destiny. Many times people have more than one gift.

Today I continue to see many people demonstrating their talents in our cultural practices, ceremonies, medicines, storytelling, music, visual and traditional arts, dancing, writers/poets, regalia-/clothing-making, building tools like paddles and canoes, languages, traditional leadership and so much more!

We are fortunate that our ancestors have held on to these gifts and passed them down to us and future generations. When we rebuild our Nations, we have what we need, and there is no shortage of what needs to be done. To accomplish the rebuilding of our Nations, you must figure out what your gift is and share that with the world. When you feel inspired, joyful, and energetic, you will know you have tapped into your gift. kayās (*a long time ago*), Elders in the communities would know who was gifted in what way. They would take that child to certain people with those specialties and the children would be their helpers while they were mentored to eventually be 'experts' in an area.

miyo-ohpikihāwasowin

Good Child-Rearing

What I offer here is based on teachings that I have heard over time from my family, friends, and Elders. If I am to make any mistakes, they are my own. From what I understand, our communities were once very child centered. Children were protected, disciplined, and nurtured by everyone in the community. miyo-pimātisiwin[12] was taught right from the beginning.

There were ceremonies and songs sung for many reasons: to ask for a child to be born, its birth, burying his/her umbilical cord and placenta, name-giving, and walking. There are probably many more that I am unaware of. When news of pregnancy came, a community celebrated and they were ecstatic, but they were also careful not to do things too soon, for a spirit could decide to go back home to the spirit world.

Before children were born, a mother was to be mindful of her thoughts, words, and actions because she held in her womb a sacred being tied to the spiritual world. Men were to treat them with the utmost kindness and were careful not to hurt them emotionally. This practice was intended to make sure that the child born felt wanted, loved, protected, and peaceful. ēkā ta-mātoskit.[13] Babies and toddlers spent their time with their mothers. They were nurtured and loved by them and by older siblings. They were carried around on cradleboards and in moss-bags so they could observe the world through their eyes first. This practice made sure ēkā ta-āyimisit;[14] this made them quite clever and respectful. Lullabies of love and endearment were sung to them in Cree as they swung in swings made especially for babies. The swing was used to provide a sense of being back in the womb. Safe, loved, and protected.

A child grew up to be respectful of everyone because they were taught to be mindful of their behaviour and not to be disrespectful because it was understood and signalled to be one of our Natural laws, and there were many. An Elder also taught me that a child grows up to his/her maximum potential when raised this way. Parents were also not to interfere with the child's path in life, and they were taught to respect its autonomy. Children have their own personalities, challenges, and paths in life. If we were to try to control the child's life path, we would have stepped over our own teachings and boundaries. This could lead to a hard life for the child as they grow to be adults. For example, if our child expresses his/her identity as two-spirit or chooses a specific profession, and if we as parents try to control their choice by trying to force them to be something else, we have interfered and have caused them turmoil and difficulty.

Another example that is useful for today is discipline. Everyone in the community was involved with the discipline of a child. This ensured respectful behaviour and that they were abiding by the Natural laws. When a parent interferes with that discipline, we are leading them away from miyo-pimātisiwin, or a good path in life. ē-pāstāhacik,[15] teaching them that the Natural laws do not apply to them. This can cause suffering for the child, the parents, or children yet to come.

Our ability to parent our children this way was one of the things attacked by the government and churches. They achieved this by taking the children out of the lands, away from their kinship systems and communities. Our families were unable to practise their teachings of traditional child-rearing. Some residential school survivors were unable to love and felt unworthy; their spirits were tainted by the ugliness of the people that came to change who they were born to be. A sad result is what we see today; we can see it in the statistics of high suicide rates, high incarceration rates, addictions and poverty—heart-wrenching consequences of the residential school era.

Fortunately, this is beginning to turn around. People are realizing that our teachings are worth remembering and practising. Today I witness many people on social media making good efforts to teach their child about miyo-pimātisiwin. Children are dancing, singing, being taught to speak their language, experiencing ceremonies, beading, arts, cultural and land-based practices such as picking medicines, hunting, fishing, and much more. Women are picking up the teachings of traditional child-rearing, having name-giving ceremonies and walking ceremonies. Parents, grandparents, aunties, uncles, and cousins understand that they are the key in the transmission of miyo-pimātisiwin and language. It is so beautiful to witness! Our ancestors did not fight for us in vain after all; that is the legacy they left for us. Now it is up to us to determine what legacy we will leave for our future generations.

The next part of the book is the practical application of nēhiyawēwin in the home. It does not contain a comprehensive list of activities that you can do with your child—that would be next to impossible. However, Belinda and I have tried our very best to provide you with the language that is or can be useful to use with your child as you begin to reclaim your language with your children.

PART THREE

sōskwāc ta-āpacihtāyēk nēhiyawēwin kīkiwāhk

The Practical Application of Cree in the Home

CHAPTER ONE

okāwīmāw ōma niya

.... 🍓 ....

I Am a Mother

Before we begin, we position ourselves as mothers and caregivers of our homes, as this is our role and responsibility, as is the transmission of our language to our children. It is our natural duty and our sacred law. This language revitalization and reclamation effort comes from a place of heart and real practice; we want to share, as it comes from mothering our children in Cree.

By transmitting our Cree language to our children, we are reclaiming our mothering domain, which is not easy but is empowering when made into a habit with family-focus and effort. This is self-determination and sovereignty in practice. We offer something special. Andrea is a fluent speaker and Belinda is a second-language learner; with our combined efforts we offer an expertise that is second to none. We also visit and our children see us engage and speak Cree to each other, which is the best mothering and mentoring that can exist. We keep family in mind throughout this book, for future generations.

> ANDREA: I have been working on teaching my eleven-year-old daughter the Cree language since 2013 and immersing my three-year-old son since birth. I find it much easier to teach Cree to my son who is just learning a language. Teaching my daughter, on the other hand, has been more challenging. She understands a great deal of Cree, sounds like she's a fluent speaker when she does speak but does so minimally. I am always looking for ways to improve my methodologies and maintain momentum.
>
> When Belinda and I met in Prince Albert, we discussed the idea of a manual for other families to use to begin speaking Cree in their homes. This guide is the result of that discussion. Together, Belinda and I hope to bring forth an invaluable tool for families who wish to make the Cree language the language of their home.
>
> We (Andrea and Belinda) first shared and discussed the idea of this manual over coffee in a quiet little restaurant on the west hill of Prince Albert, Saskatchewan, at one time referred to as the 'meeting place': kistapinānhik, a meeting place where our ancestors frequently visited and camped some time in the not-too-distant past.

okāwīmāw ōma niya | I Am a Mother

We are both language activists and teachers of Cree language and want to ensure it is passed on through our families. This is our contribution to the future of Cree people.

BELINDA: I have been working on language recovery and reclamation since the beginning of my career as an educator. Like Andrea, I started thinking deeply about the Cree language when I was a young mother. Ryan, my third-born son, who was born during the millennium year, was my motivation and anchor to move into language learning. This was the start of my journey as an adult second-language learner. I have written numerous personalized journals of my language recovery, language learning and its meaning, the contexts of language acquisition, and terminology needed to get to where I wanted to go. As a long-time journal writer, I still have these accounts, which will be useful in writing this manual for others to bring nēhiyawēwin home. I continue to speak nēhiyawēwin at home with my youngest daughter, Lily.

This manual is intended to be 'easy,' accessible, and for everyday learners who want to start learning Cree and make it 'a mission' of reclamation for their home.

CHAPTER TWO

mācihtātān

Let's Begin

Language revitalization begins in the home. As caregivers, we are charged with the sacred duty of raising our children in a good way. This includes giving them a part of their identities as nēhiyawak that is central to their cultural foundation, the foundation which all our ancestors once stood on and which has been passed down through the generations. The world view embedded into the Cree language is the key in which lies our understanding of how we should carry ourselves in this world. Becoming active in revitalizing language in your home is one of the greatest gifts you can give your child. As mothers and experienced Cree language teachers, this manual was developed to help you do just that; today is a good day to start.

ANDREA: Some days it is a challenge to revitalize the Cree language in your home. There are different problems you can sometimes encounter, so we must find ways to stay motivated. It is at these times that you need to look within to find and articulate the reasons behind wanting to learn Cree and passing it on to your child. Staying focused on your reasons will get you through. "What are we fighting for?" an Elder replied to me when I asked him why it was important for us to continue with our language work. I had been seeking answers for my own inspiration and motivation because, at times, I feel overwhelmed and discouraged. His reply made me ponder about the value of the Cree language and why it is so important to pass it on to our children.

I realized that I did not truly understand the significance of our Cree language. Later I came to realize that our language offers a pathway to living a good life and it holds clues as to how Cree societies should be structured and lived. I also came to understand that it is one of the key identifiers of Nationhood and identity, that Cree connects me to the world of my ancestors, and lastly, it was passed down to me from previous generations. I owe it to my ancestors, grandparents, parents, children, and any future grandchildren and great-grandchildren to continue passing the language on, so I set out to pass on this gift to them. We are fighting for our past, present, and future, and it is a worthy cause.

In our home, both my husband and I are fluent speakers. Scarlett, my youngest daughter, learned English first and Cree second. Andrew, my last-born child, is currently immersed in Cree so that it becomes his first language. He is not speaking yet, but he understands many Cree words. It is exciting to witness his language growth and I am looking forward to hearing him use what he's been learning since birth. I use second-language teaching methods with Scarlett; it can be quite challenging to stay in Cree because there is that language barrier and communication in Cree can be strained. At times, I use Total Physical Response (TPR; see Chapter 4), real objects, or images, or I model to show her what I'm talking about. We also use memory aids such as a whiteboard and flashcards. I love giving her high fives or hugs when she says or remembers a word; this shows her that I am proud of her progress and it encourages her to continue trying.

BELINDA: Learning nēhiyawēwin as an adult second-language learner has not been an easy task, but it has been a rewarding one nonetheless. As a young person, I always felt fragmented and not whole, and I attribute this feeling and realization to being a result of mainstream education and the colonial curriculum. My needs as a young nēhiyaw woman were not being met in a colonial-structured high school. This is where I truly felt the notions of not belonging and felt aspects of my identity ignored.

Later in life, as an adult, I came back full circle, back to school, this time as an educator. I soon realized that in the mainstream education system I could not teach the way I believed in, a way that honours the identity of, and shares the ways of knowing and being of a nēhiyaw, an Exact body, Cree. I am forced to teach in a way that is uncomfortable for me, in an authoritarian way, and as a new teacher I was told to teach students as students and not as friends or family. I then was chosen to teach Cree as a core subject. At the time I had no inkling of how to do this and looked to my nōhkom (*my grandmother*) and other Cree-speaking teachers for guidance.

I started exploring other ways of teaching and learning the language. If I felt this way—fragmented and unsure of my Creeness—I can imagine so many others like myself did so too. I was in search of the Cree language within me and my surroundings. This is where the nēhiyawak language experience was instructive. I started an annual summer language camp that runs in the month of July, where learners like myself could truly live in a nēhiyaw way. This gathering place was also in my home community, and we were doing exactly what our ancestors have always done. In 2000, I had my son Ryan, my language anchor. I had nōhkom, who represented the gateway of the past, and she was my access to the animacy of the Cree language of the present. My future has been this: bringing language learners along with me, with us. nēhiyawak ōma kiyānaw.[16] This manual is just that: bringing you along with us.

Assessing Your Situation

First, you must determine your household language abilities, as each will have their own unique journey. There are three common approaches to or contexts for passing on the language to children:

1) PARENTS AS FLUENT SPEAKERS
   People might assume that because both parents are fluent they would know how to pass on the language to their child. However, times have changed, and English is quite dominant. There are a few strategies that parents can try if their children are not yet speaking nēhiyawēwin and have picked up English as their dominant language. The second-language acquisition methodologies are listed in Chapter 4. One of the goals for fluent speakers that should be highlighted is "normalizing" Cree in the home. This is more challenging than it seems; you must

always be dedicated and remind each other to stay in the language. Children will pick up on the sounds, meanings, nuances, and language as they hear you speak only Cree around them. Also, use the methods listed in Chapter 4. If they are newborns, teach and talk to them in Cree only. Do not talk to them in any language other than Cree. English will be picked up eventually quite easily, as they will hear it on television, from people around them, from family members who do not know Cree, etc. You can also remind visitors who speak the language to speak Cree to your child, perhaps even putting up a sign that says "nēhiyawēwin only beyond this door," at the very least for fluent speakers; non-speakers can try and learn. Lastly, try your best every day. Some days you will slip and that's okay. Start over again. It'll come naturally in time. āhkamēyimok.

2) ONE PARENT, ONE LANGUAGE (OPOL)
The idea behind one parent, one language is that the fluent speaker in the home speaks only that language to your child. The other one speaks the dominant language. The child will grow to know both languages. Children are very good at distinguishing the sounds and meanings of both, and evidence states that they will not become confused but will grow up fluent speakers of both languages. They will be able to speak

and think in both languages, transitioning from one language to the next flawlessly.

3) PARENTS AS LEARNERS OF THE LANGUAGE
In this situation, neither of the parents speak the language, so they must learn it as a family. Studies have shown that children growing up in this type of household grow up to be better speakers than their parents. Imagine that! This book will certainly help you get started. The journey to reclaiming your language will be challenging but fulfilling. Find what works best for you and your family and build on it. Finally, stay determined—āhkamēyimok.

For more information on these language situations, refer to Leanne Hinton's *Bringing Our Languages Home*.[17]

CHAPTER THREE

osihtā pīkiskwēwin kaskihtāwina

Setting Language Goals

Setting goals for yourself and your family is important. It makes your language-learning mission more manageable, and you will feel successful with each word, phrase, and area you learn. A language bank is a visual representation of the vocabulary and phrases that you have made and learned. Seeing your progress helps you assess your language growth and, most importantly, it helps you stay motivated.

Set time aside to keep Cree spoken and listened to—anywhere from five minutes to one hour daily for the first month, or year. It is said, 1,000 hours in the language or learning a language will get you to beginner proficiency; 3,000 hours will lead to intermediate vocabulary proficiency.

Once you learn a word or phrase in Cree, make it a point to never use that word in English again.

Note the strategies and methods that work best for you and your family. For example, in my (Andrea's) family, I always ask to be repeated after I have introduced a word. Once my family members know the word, I will not reply until asked in Cree. I also praise my children when they use the Cree language.

Studies show that people can learn five—plus or minus two—words at a time. You can use this number in your goal setting. Use the SMART approach to goal setting: Specific, Measurable, Achievable, Realistic, and Time-Bound.

EXAMPLE: September—learn:
- Seven terms for family
- Seven nouns
- Seven verbs
- Seven food terms

OR

- Prayer
- Song

Take your daily routine into consideration. This is the time you are spending with your child/family; think about what vocabulary you need in that time span—when you're eating breakfast, cleaning up, getting dressed, doing homework, reading books, shopping, going for a car ride and going to bed. What other activities do you do with your child?

What vocabulary do you need for that activity? Make these your language-learning goals.

Consider bathroom terminology, for example: what is the vocabulary that I need to feel that I've reached my goal for that room? I can say: *bathroom*; *I need to use the bathroom*; *brush your teeth*; *brush your hair*; *do you need to pee?*; *have a bath/shower*, etc. The terms used most often are provided to you in the vocabulary section. After you have learned most of the vocabulary that is related to the bathroom you can move to a different area, such as your car, or you can challenge them all around the same time. This is the method that I use at home. It provides more consistency and once a word is known in the language, I try my best not to use it in English again.

CHAPTER FOUR

kā-miyo-āpatahki kīkwaya

Methods

There are many ways (methods) for learning a language: Immersion, Direct Method, Natural Approach, Total Physical Response (TPR), Accelerated Second Language Acquisition (ASLA), Task-Based Language Learning Method, and Grammar.

> Language learning is different from acquisition. Language learning is 'knowing the rules,' having a conscious knowledge about grammar. . . . Language learning is not nearly as important in **developing communicative ability in a second language**.[18]

Becoming familiar with various types of methods when learning a language is essential. Learning about teaching and transmitting a language is also useful because fluency is not enough. Learners have to be trained to learn and must know when to take advantage of opportunities, and have a responsibility to assist in their own learning. Learners have to be trained to learn.

Immersion is the best method, but when that is not attainable, here are some other approaches we found useful. When learning to speak Cree, the most effective way is to do so in a natural process.

> Learning has be done mutually by the learner and the teacher. If one party does not have the motivation to learn, the learning cannot take place, nor can learning take place out of context, that is by talking English when Cree is the language to be learned.[19]

A. THE DIRECT METHOD means no translation allowed. The speaker has to demonstrate, role play, and act out phrases to get the meaning across and communicate in the target language. Visual aides are also used, along with real life objects. The learning takes place through experience in real-world contexts, like mealtime, bath time, or going for a visit with a relative. The Direct Method uses a lot of real-life vocabulary. Oral transmission is carefully built up and then questions are introduced along with answers. Sentence use is emphasized. Speech and listening are all a part of this process. Learners will learn to self-correct. The only criticized drawback is it is dependent on the 'skill' of the teacher/speaker. For more on the Direct Method, look for François Gouin, then later Maximilian D. Berlitz and Lambert Sauveur. Reading and writing are also a part of this approach; however, that will come later.

B. THE NATURAL APPROACH is based on Krashen's Naturalistic Theory. It is similar to the Direct Method but different in that this approach is based on a beginner level of communication.

C. TOTAL PHYSICAL RESPONSE (TPR) is an extension of the Natural Approach modified by James Ashton. TPR is an effective approach to assist learners to understand the sounds of words and focused on direction. TPR relies on providing direction in verbal commands for learners to respond to after closely listening and watching. Learners will repeat after the speaker. Learners act on command. The household is a good place to start with this method. Mothers and fathers often will tell their children to put shoes away, do the dishes, take a shower, etc. This is as natural as it comes for parenting, of course in a loving way.

D. THE ACCELERATED SECOND LANGUAGE ACQUISITION METHOD was developed by Neyooxet Greymorning. This method is based on images and pictures of different things going on in the snapshot. Pictures start off as simple and move to more complex 'happenings' in the images. Simple images include a woman, a girl, a boy, a man, an elderly woman, an elderly man, etc. Then images move into more complex images of people doing different things that are relevant to the teacher and learner as a team in their context.

The ASLA method applies brain science, using hundreds of images to create a context and to inundate the learner with various images in the language. Pictures are broken down into skill sets to learn the target vocabulary without any English translation. These are taught with very little repetition. This effective method teaches language using cognition, meaning direct communication with no translation of English used. This method is also useful using blocks of time, such as minutes to hours, in a day or week.

This is a highly effective method that one needs to be trained in to thoroughly understand and effectively apply. Look for Dr. Greymorning workshops near you.

E. TASK-BASED LANGUAGE LEARNING takes place when learners are working in relevant contexts. Tasks are meaningful with clear outcomes. Examples of tasks can include: mealtime, bath time, and 'getting ready for school,' or perhaps a scene from a movie or book. Task-based language learning involves teaching with a communicative approach that is authentic and practical.

F. GRAMMAR-BASED TRANSLATION. In contemporary society, we do not have easy access to communities that are entirely Cree-speaking nor do we always have access to fluent speakers. Therefore, in Cree, it is an important skill to recognize and understand how the language functions to assist you in your learning. Picking up the patterns that are used in the Standard Roman Orthography will assist greatly in pronunciation and identification of the function of the language.

This guide offers a minimal introduction to some basics of Cree grammar, such as the Cree sound system, gender (animate and inanimate), and number (singular and plural), along with vocabulary used around the home and 100 high-frequency words to be used at your own discretion.

G. AUDIO. You can listen to Cree audio while you sleep or while you are driving so that you can pick up on sounds, gauge what you know, and learn the nuances of the language.

CHAPTER FIVE

āpacihcikana

Resources

Resources, resources, resources! You need them. Luckily, many people have been at this for quite some time, so now we have a ton of material available for us. When I (Andrea) first started teaching Cree as a second language to my daughter, I found that I needed resources. Some are free, some are bought, and some I made. Please note that the list provided is not an exhaustive list. Find what you love using.

PEOPLE: Who are the fluent speakers around you? Who can you visit? Is there a local Cree-speaking group you can join? Who can you ask to help your child? Maybe it's an aunt, uncle, cousin, or grandparent. You can go visit them. Listening to fluent speakers in conversation is like music to the ears, and the spirit recognizes this. I don't know about you, but it makes me quite happy to hear fluent speakers having conversations. Personally, when I am away from my son, I ask a fluent speaker to watch my son and speak Cree to him. This way I'm ensuring that he has Cree input throughout the day.

MUSIC: There is a lot of music available on Spotify, YouTube, and on iTunes that is available for download and viewing. Kids love songs, singing, and dancing, which makes it easier for them to listen to the language. Songs are also known to 'stick' to the brain, so children remember them long after they've heard them. Some I recommend are Darlene Auger's Cree lullabies and Brian MacDonald's Cree songs. The Cree lullabies by Auger are a great resource for baby's naptime: they are soothing and you can learn how to sing the lyrics for your child. Brian MacDonald's Cree songs are great for singing along to on your road trips![20]

BOOKS: Books are a great resource because they are repetitive—they don't change, so children will pick up on the vocabulary used in the book and the context it is used in. It is also a meaningful way to spend time and bond with your child. It is sākihitowin in action. There are many books available written in syllabics and nēhiyaw Standard Roman Orthography and some written in both nēhiyawēwin and English.

1) I started with level readers from Eagle Crest books, and they are written in nēhiyawēwin.

āpacihcikana | *Resources*

2) I also like the work of Celia Deschambault's level readers.[21] They are easy to follow and provide learners with beginning vocabulary. The only caution I have for some of these books is that the Standard Roman Orthography is tailored for their respective regions.

3) The most useful tool is to ensure that you have a dictionary written in Cree Standard Roman Orthography. The most comprehensive one I have is Arok Wolvengrey's *nēhiyawēwin itwēwina* or *Cree: Words*. Since the vocabulary listed in our guide is not comprehensive of the entire Cree language, this dictionary is a great tool to have when you need a word.

4) Solomon Ratt's *māci-nēhiyawēwin* is a textbook that includes numerous exercises with images and instructions on using the textbook. It is fairly easy to understand, giving learners a good foundation on how Cree functions and how to use nouns, verbs, and person indicators properly with the paradigms provided.

5) Jean Okimāsis's *Cree: Language of the Plains* textbook and accompanying workbook are available for free as PDFs for those language

enthusiasts who are motivated to learn the grammar of the language. This will help you understand and learn nēhiyawēwin. You can find it on creeliteracy.org or search Jean Okimāsis *Cree: Language of the Plains*. A revised version has also been published and is available for purchase in bookstores across the country and online.

WEBSITES: There is an abundance of information out there in the virtual world that is waiting for us to discover and use. It was all made for people like us—hungry to learn nēhiyawēwin—and they've done so much amazing work! Here are a few that I have found online:

1) **creeliteracy.org** offers a wealth of resources written in Cree Standard Roman Orthography. There are videos spoken in Cree, blogs written about Cree, and stories both contemporary and sacred. If you want an online site that has a bit of everything, this is the site you want to visit!

2) **littlecreebooks.com** provides online books that can be printed for your child. They are colourful and easy to follow along. They are offered in both nēhiyaw SRO and syllabics or both.

3) **learncreewithandrea.com** is my own site. I've created a blog section where you can watch videos of my friends and family as I share my language revitalization journey with my own children and others.

4) **creeclass.com** is authored by Bill Cook, a Cree language instructor who's worked in Cree language education for over fourteen years in various capacities. He has an abundance of resources listed on his site, including audio files, handouts, quizzes, and videos!

FACEBOOK SITES: Social media is rich with people who are eager to share what they know about the nēhiyaw language. You are also able to connect with the larger community of people who are interested in learning along with you. There are a few that I am most familiar with: (nēhiyawēwin) Cree Word of the Day, Cree Language Videos, and Cree Simon Says.

RADIO: MBC radio is one of my favourite stations. It features some of the Michif and Woodland Cree spoken in northern, northeast, and north-central Saskatchewan. And what a treat it is to listen to stories of long ago as told by featured Elders and Knowledge Keepers.[22]

APPS: As we move forward in contemporary society, it is more attractive for students to use the technology available to them. We can use this to our advantage by providing our children with access to apps that offer nēhiyawēwin resources. I've only included a few here; feel free to search "Cree" for your apps.

1) Cree Dictionary is my absolute favourite app. When I need a word in nēhiyawēwin or want to know how to spell a word properly in nēhiyaw SRO it is my go-to app. Arok Wolvengrey Standard Roman Orthography is the one I use first. If there is no word provided by him, I then use the other words that are provided. Sometimes, my daughter will ask me how to say a word in Cree, then she goes on this app to see if I said it properly or if there is more than one way to say a word.

2) Cree File Hills Qu'Appelle Tribal Council (FHQTC) has an app available that includes twenty-three categories. It includes images, pronunciation guides, and quizzes to keep your child challenged.

3) First Nations Storybook: Bush Cree has a series of books available in the app. Children can follow along as the story is read.

This book will also provide a few of the resources that I have created and use at home.

CHAPTER SIX

ka-ayamihtāhk nēhiyawasinahikēwin

Reading Cree Standard Roman Orthography

In this section, you will learn about Cree Standard Roman Orthography that is used for the Cree language, with the goal to have you become independent learners. Learning any language requires you, as a learner, to understand that each language has its own range of sounds, including Cree, so it is important that you put aside your knowledge of the English alphabet and its sounds.

There are three parts: (1) the Cree consonants and their sounds, (2) the Cree vowel sounds and understanding the use of the macron or circumflex that is often used to mark a long vowel sound, and finally, (3) breaking down the syllables to help sound out long words using clapping as a method.[23]

1. There are ten consonants: p, t, k, c, s, h, m, n, y, w.

Most consonants in Cree sound like their English counterparts, but there are four consonants that have a unique sound: p, t, k, and c.

- /p/ is a cross between a /p/ and a /b/. Using your lips and voice, try sounding this out. You should not hear a sharp /p/ or /b/ but a sound that is in between the two sounds. Note: It sounds like the /p/ in English when it is the final sound in a word. Example: hop.

- /t/ is a cross between a /t/ and a /d/. Using your tongue and voice, try sounding this out. You should not hear a sharp /t/ or a /d/ but a sound that is in between the two sounds. Note: It sounds like the /t/ in English when it is the final sound in a word. Example: hot.

- /k/ is a cross between a /k/ and a /g/. Using the middle of your tongue and your voice, touch the top of your mouth towards the back and try sounding this out. You should not hear a sharp /k/ or a /g/ sound but a sound that is in between the two. Note: It sounds like the /k/ in English when it is the final sound in a word. Example: hawk.

- /c/ has two distinct sounds, depending on the speaker. It either makes a /ts/ or /ch/ sound—you can use your teeth and tongue to make either sound. It never makes a /k/ sound as its English counterpart may sometimes do.

This consonant chart is provided to you as an example and for your own reference

Consonant	Initial	Medial	Final
/p/	**p**ahkisimon *sunset*	kis**p**ēwātam *he/she defends it*	sīsī**p** *duck*
/t/	**t**ahkāw *it is cold*	ō**t**ē *over here*	ē-tēpwē**t** *he/she yells*
/k/	**k**īsta *you too*	ayī**k**is *frog*	ayis**k** *because*
/c/	**c**ahkās *ice cream*	ko**c**ihtāw *he/she tries*	māskō**c** *likely*
/s/	**s**askan *it is melting*	ka**s**kihtāw *he/she is able to*	tāwicihcī**s** *middle finger*
/h/	**h**ā *Who? What?*	a**h**cahk *Spirit*	ī**h** *look*
/m/	**m**ītihp *brain*	pa**m**ihēw *he/she takes care of*	macasti**m** *bad dog*
/n/	**n**itōsis *my aunt*	tā**n**ita *where*	kīspi**n** *if*
/y/	**y**āwēw *heard in a distance*	ā**y**iman *it is difficult*	nipi**y** *water*
/w/	**w**īsopiy *gall bladder*	sōsk**w**āc *just*	māto**w** *he/she cries*

2. There are four vowels: i, o, a, ē.

There are both short and long vowels, making a combination of seven different vowel sounds. Oftentimes a macron or a circumflex is used to mark the long vowel. Below, you will see that the macron is used to mark the length of the vowel as long.

- /i/ sounds like the **i** in 'it'

- /a/ sounds like the first **a** in 'appeal'

- /o/ sounds like the **oo** in 'took'

- /ī/ sounds like the **ee** in 'see'

- /ā/ sounds like the **a** in 'fat'

- /ō/ sounds like the **oo** in 'tooth'

- /ē/ sounds like the **ay** in 'day '

ka-ayamihtāhk nēhiyawasinahikēwin | *Reading Cree SRO*

This vowel chart is provided to you as an example and for your own reference

Vowel	Initial	Medial	Final
/a/	**a**siskiy *dirt*	m**a**ci *bad*	mān**a** *usually*
/ā/	**ā**hāsiw *crow*	w**ā**wi *egg*	k**ā** *oh!*
/ē/	**ē**sis *seashell*	p**ē**ci *to here*	nōsis**ē** *grandchild*
/i/	**i**tohtēwin *goal of journey*	p**i**miy *lard/butter*	pāsic**i** *stepping over*
/ī/	**ī**hī *yes*	k**ī**hk**ī**hk *in spite*	c**ī** *question marker*
/o/	**o**cēk *fisher*	nīs**o**tak *two canoes*	kākit**o** *be quiet*
/ō/	**ō**si *boat*	n**ō**makēs *for a while*	ahp**ō** *or*

3. Clapping is a method used to help with pronunciation and improve accent.

In Part Three you will be given some words to practise. I suggest you clap to each syllable; as you get better at it, try it faster; and then eventually try it without the clapping and breaking the syllables up for a smoother pronunciation.

NOTE: Each syllable is often separated at the vowel, as you will see in the following examples.

api (sit) = two syllables	a + pi	two claps
mīciso (eat) = three syllables	mī + ci + so	three claps
kawisimo (go to bed) = four syllables	ka + wi + si + mo	four claps
masinahikē (write) = five syllables	ma + si + na + hi + kē	five claps

Try it on your own. Find words that you want to learn and can break up into syllables, and then add your clapping method. After some practice, ask a fluent speaker if you are on the right track.

ka–ayamihtāhk nēhiyawasinahikēwin | *Reading Cree SRO*

| Cree Word | Break into syllables | # of claps |

| Cree Word | Break into syllables | # of claps |

| Cree Word | Break into syllables | # of claps |

| Cree Word | Break into syllables | # of claps |

| Cree Word | Break into syllables | # of claps |

| Cree Word | Break into syllables | # of claps |

CHAPTER SEVEN

ka-nēhiyawēyan kīkihk

Speaking Cree Around the Home

If you are teaching Cree or learning Cree with your family, use any and all opportunities to speak Cree to the children throughout the day. Remember that children are born with the ability to learn any language. With this in mind, the language you speak to them is the one they will learn to understand and speak. Bilingual households are also an added feature when it comes to the brain and its function. The brain is hardwired for multiple languages.

Begin by talking to the children in complete phrases and sentences. Even if you think they do not understand what you are saying, speak anyway. Demonstrate. What is also important to note is that children and learners are also learning the rhythm, the nuances, and the pronunciations of the Cree language. Talk to other people who are fluent speakers in the language, and encourage the language to be spoken in the household with all who live and enter your home. Make it the Cree-speaking zone if at all possible, or mark out the time of when this is to be done. Make it a challenge with other auntie and uncle households.

Now, when it comes to the specifics of topics in the language and use of it, think about what language you would normally use, for example, when cooking or taking a walk, cleaning up parts of the house, changing a diaper, or getting ready to go to school or to the movies. Think about what the weather is like or how a certain person is doing, etc., and use that vocabulary with the children.

The next few chapters cover the following topics:

- Cree vocabulary

- 100 high-frequency words

- Suggested activities

I highly suggest that you transfer any of the activities suggested into journals that include drawings and the terms or take pictures of you and your family. You can also make videos or scrapbooks and add the text. These are ways learners can deepen their learning and assess and record their language reclamation journey.

CHAPTER EIGHT

nēhiyawēwin itwēwina

Cree Vocabulary

The following pages provide some examples of vocabulary you can use on a daily basis. As you get used to using Cree daily, add more to your vocabulary and invite your loved ones, relatives, and Elders to teach you words you may be unfamiliar with.

Once you can say and understand a word in Cree, never use it in English again!

NOTE:
NA—Noun Animate
NI—Noun Inanimate
SG—Singular
PL—Plural

nēhiyawētān kīkinähk | *Speaking Cree in the Home*

atamiskākēwin ēkwa pīkiskwēwin / Greetings and Conversations	
Hello, how are you?	tānisi!
Good morning	miyo-kīkisēpāyaw
Come in	pē-pīhtikwē
Take off your shoes ... coat ... hat ... mitts	kētaskisinē kētasākē kētastotinē kētastisē
Put on your shoes ... coat ... hat ... mitts	postaskisinē postasākē postastotinē postastisē
Hang up your coat	akotā kiskotākay
Put away your shoes ... hat ... mitts	nāhastā kimaskisina nāhastā kitastotin nahāhik kitastisak
Go and sit down	nitawi-api
Thank you	kinanāskomitin (SG) kinanāskomitināwāw (PL)
Tell me a story	ācimostawin
What have you been up to?	tānisi ē-kī-itahkamikisiyan?

nēhiyawēwin itwēwina | *Cree Vocabulary*

How was your day?	tānisi kikī-isi-kīsikanisin?
I had a good day	nikī-miyo-kīsikanisin
I had a bad day	nikī-maci-kīsikanisin
Hug me	ākwaskitinin
I need a hug	ninōhtē-ākwaskitinikawin
Yes	āha/ēha
No	namōya
I do not know	namōya nikiskēyihtēn
I think so	ēkosi pakahkam

itwēwina kicawāsicimis ohci / Words to Use with Your Child	
Sit down	api
Sing	nikamo
Come here	āstam
Eat	mīciso
Clean up	nāhastāso
Stay still	koskwāwātapi kiyāmapi
Listen	natohta
Read	ayamihcikē
Write	masinahikē
Let's get ready	mamanētān
Let's go	ēkwa
Clean up	nāhastāso kinipāwikamikohk
Tidy up (general)	nāhastāso

nēhiyawēwin itwēwina | *Cree Vocabulary*

mīcisonāniwina / *Meal Times*

Sit down	api
Are you hungry?	kinōhtēhkatān cī?
Do you want more?	kiyāpic cī?
Yes, I'm hungry	āha, ninōhtēhkatān ōma
No, I'm not hungry	namwāc, namōya ninōhtēhkatān
Does this food taste good?	wīhkasin cī? (NI) wīhkitisow cī? (NA)
Are you full?	kikīspon cī?
Yes, I'm full	aha, nikīspon ōma
Come and eat	āstam, pē-mīciso
Pass the salt … pepper	pē-itisina sīwīhtākan pē-itisina papēskomina
Are you thirsty?	kinōhtēyāpākwan cī?
Do you want to drink water? … milk? … juice? … coffee?	kinōhtē-minihkwān cī nipiy? kinōhtē-minihkwān cī tohtōsāpoy? kinōhtē-minihkwān cī sīwāpos? kinōhtē-minihkwān cī pīh-kāhtēwāpoy?
Is it yummy?	wīhkasin cī? (NI) wīhkitisow cī? (NA)
Does it taste bad?	macispakwan cī? (NI) macispakosow cī? (NA)
Eat your vegetables	mīci anihi kikīscikānisa

piminawasowikamik—masinahikē kipiminawasowikamik / Kitchen—Label Your Kitchen	
Dish (bowl or plate)	oyākan
Cup	minihkwākan
Knife	mōhkomān
Spoon	ēmihkwān
Fork	cīstahasēpon
Cupboard	akocikan
Fridge	tahkascikan
Stove	kotawānāpisk
Frying pan	napwēn
Table	mīcisowināhtik
Chair	tēhtapiwin

nipāwin ahpō nipāsiwin / Sleep or Nap Time

Are you tired?	kinōhtēhkwasin cī?
Lie down	pimisini
Close your eyes	pasakwāpi
Go to sleep	nipā
It's time to wake up	waniskā
Did you have a good sleep?	kikī-miyohkwāmin cī? kikī-miyonipān cī?
Are you still tired?	kiyāpic cī kinōhtēhkwasin?
Bed	nipēwin
Pillow	apaskwēsimon
Blanket	akohp
Do you want a blanket?	kinitawēyimāw cī akohp?
I am sleepy/tired	ninōhtēhkwasin
Dream	pawāta
I had a dream	nikī-pawātēn
I had a good dream	nikī-miyo-pawātēn
I had a bad dream	nikī-kostācihkwāmin
Time for bed	nitawi-kawisimo ēkwa

nēhiyawētān kīkināhk | *Speaking Cree in the Home*

akayāskamohtahiwē itwēwina / Introductory Vocabulary	
What's your name?	tānisi kitisiyihkāson?
My name is _____	_____ nitisiyihkāson
Where are you from?	tānitē ōma ohci kiya?
I am from _____	_____ ōma ohci niya
Who is your mom?	awīna ana kimāmā? awīna ana kikāwiy? (Old Cree)
_____ is my mom	_____ nimāmā _____ nikāwiy
Who is your dad?	awīna ana kipāpā? awīna ana kohtāwiy? (Old Cree)
_____ is my dad	_____ nipāpā _____ nohtāwiy
How old are you?	tānitāhtopiponēyan? (Old Cree) tānitāhtwāskīwinēyan? (New Cree)
I am _____ years old.	_____ nititāhtopiponān _____ nititahtwāskēwinān
What is this?	kīkwāy ōma?
This is _____	_____ ōma
Where is the _____?	tānawē _____? (NI) tānawā _____? (NA)
_____ is here (NI) _____ is here (NA)	macik-ōmita (NI) macik-owīta
Say this	omisi itwī
What are you doing?	kīkwāy ī-itōtaman?
I am _____ (e.g., I am eating or I am playing)	_____ ōma ē-mīcisoyān ōma ē-mētawēyān ōma

mīsīwīkamikohk / In the Bathroom	
Wash your hands	kāsīcihcē
Wash your face	kāsīhkwē
Brush your teeth	kisīpēkāpitē
Wipe yourself	kimisāho
Flush it	kotāwipaha kotāwina
Dry your hands	pāhkocihcēho
Toilet	mīsīwikamik
Toilet paper	kimisāhowinēkin
I need some toilet paper!	ninitawēyihtēn kimisāhowinēkin
Towel	kāsīhkwākan
I need a towel	ninitawēyihtēn kāsīhkwākan
Where are the towels?	tāniwēhā kāsīhkwākana
Water	nipiy
The water is hot	kisākamitēw ōma nipiy
The water is cold	tahkikamin ōma nipiy
Don't use too much water	kāya mistahi āpacihtā nipiy
Dry yourself off	pāhkwahisow

nēhiyawētān kīkinãhk | Speaking Cree in the Home

wayawītimihk / Outdoors	
What's the weather like today?	kā-isi-kīsikāk anohc?
Are you cold?	kikawacin cī?
Are you hot?	kikīsōsin cī?
It is hot	kisāstīw
It is cold	tahkāyāw
It is very cold	kisināw
It is windy	yōtin
It is snowing	mispon
It is raining	kimiwan
It is a nice day	miyo-kīsikāw
It is not a nice day	maci-kīsikāw
It is morning	kīkisēpāyāw
It is dawn	wāpan

nēhiyawēwin itwēwina | *Cree Vocabulary*

The sun is rising	pē-sākāstēw
Moonlight	nīpāyāstēw
The moon	tipiskāwi-pīsim
The sun	kīsikāwi-pīsim
Star(s)	ahcāhkos(ak)
I am looking for ladybugs	ninitonawāwak nōsē-manicōsak
Bug(s)	manicōs(ak)
Ant(s)	ēyikos(ak)
Tree(s)	mītos(ak)
Rock(s)	asiniy(ak)

mētawēwin itwēwina / Play Vocabulary

Go and play	nitawi-mēītawē
Let's play	mētawētān
Go and play with _____	nitawi-wīcīī-mētawēm _____
Use kindness	āpacihtā kisēwātisiwin
Let's play outside	mētawētān wayawītimihk
Let's play tag	mētawētān sāminitotāk
I do not want to play	namōya ninōhtē-mētawān
S/he does not want to play	namōya nōhtē-mētawēw
Let's run	pimipahtātān
Let's hide	kāsōtān
Let's build something	osīhtātān kīkway
Let's jump	kwāskohtitān
I am jumping	nikwāskohtin

nēhiyawēwin itwēwina | *Cree Vocabulary*

Swing	wēwēpison
I am swinging	niwēwēpison
Be careful	pēyāhtakisi
Get down	nīhtāhtawē
Bike	nīsokācis
I am riding a bike	nipapāmiskawāw nīsokācis
iPad	nīmā-cikāstēpayihcikanis
Put your iPad away	nāhasta ki-nīmā-cikāstēpayih-cikanis
Gaming	cikāstēpayihcikan mētawākan
No more gaming	ēkāwiya ayiwāk mētawākē cikāstēpayihcikan mētawākan
I like gaming	nimiywēyihtēn cikāstēpayihcikan mētawākan

CHAPTER NINE

mitātahtomitanaw māwaci kā-āpatahki itwēwina

100 High-Frequency Words and Phrases

About the Word List

The following list of Cree words was adapted from the Dolch Sight Words list. However, because Cree is a language that uses animate (living) and inanimate (non-living) for gender and does not use the pronouns he/she/her/him, the list has been adapted to better suit our Cree language.

This list of words was developed and incorporated in this manual for two reasons: to help children/students become readers and writers of the Cree language, but also because these words are often used by fluent speakers. Once people know these words, they will be able to figure out the rest of the sentence being used by context. They will also be able to pick up that there are more ways than one that some words can be used. For example:

minihkwē—to drink something unidentified
ni**minihkw**ān—I drink something unidentified
ki**minihkw**ān—you drink something unidentified

About the Cree Language

One concept you and your child must master is the idea of animate (living) and inanimate (non-living) nouns: for example, nāpēw (*man*) and atim (*dog*) are animate. There are some things that you would never think are animate or inanimate, but they are, so be aware. And remember, it is okay to make mistakes. It's how we learn!

Knowing if a noun is animate or inanimate changes how some verbs are used, as you will see in the sight-word list, and you would use those words as marked.

- NA means animate noun

- NI means inanimate noun

Using Your Sight Words

There are many ways to use this list, and you will find in the activity section some ways you can teach the words to your child. You can choose any ten words to start with for one or two weeks and then add another ten every week until you have learned all of the words.

What I (Andrea) have done is hang them up on one empty wall in my daughters' room in a random order. Once we tried using a flashlight to pick out the words and she would tell me the ones she knew in Cree already and others I would have to show her through action, an image, or real objects—the last resort was an English translation. Another time, we just went through each sight-word. You can google sight-word games to play with your child at home—they may be in English, Spanish, or French, but you can always adapt them to Cree. Hey, why reinvent the wheel?!

The following 100 words are used often by fluent speakers. Once you know them you will learn through context what the speakers are talking about. Each time you understand a word, celebrate and feel proud of yourself. You are learning nēhiyawēwin!

For size (big/small) or colours which can describe an animate or inanimate noun, I use examples while I use an action and say the words in Cree. For example:

misikitiw maskwa—the bear is big (NA)
apisīsisiw maskwa—the bear is small (NA)
misāw cīman—the boat is big (NI)
apisāsin cīman—the boat is small (NI)

Note: In some instances, in the Cree column below you will see the word "ahpō," which means "or." If you see this, it means there are a couple of possible ways to say a word.

1.	and	ēkwa, ahpō mīna
2.	or	ahpō
3.	in	pīhcāyihk

4.	you	kiya
5.	that	anima (NI), ana (NA)
6.	go	niyā
7.	go outside	wayawī
8.	on top	tahkohc
9.	with	asici
10.	they	wiyawāw
11.	I/me	niya
12.	but	māka
13.	not	namōya
14.	some	ātiht
15.	what	kīkwāy
16.	all	kahkiyaw
17.	we	kiyānaw
18.	when	tānispīhk
19.	say	itwē
20.	he/she said	kī-itwēw
21.	another	kotak
22.	ask	kakwēcihkēmo
23.	be kind	kisēwātisi
24.	know	kiskēyihta
25.	live	pimātisi
26.	from	ohci
27.	after	mwēstas, ahpō pātimā
28.	he/she ate	kī-mīcisow

29.	because	ayisk, ahpō wiya
30.	boy	nāpēsis
31.	day	kīsikāw
32.	each	tahto
33.	big	misāw (NI), misikitiw (NA)
34.	black	kaskitēwāw (NI), kaskitēsiw (NA)
35.	blue	sīpihkwāw (NI), sīpihkosiw (NA)
36.	front	nīkānihk
37.	first	nīkān
38.	first time	nistam
39.	give	mēki, ahpō miy
40.	great (awesome)	takahki
41.	great (important)	kihci
42.	how do you do it?	tānisi, ahpō tānisīsi
43.	high	ispimihk
44.	low	capasis
45.	down	nīhcāyihk
46.	house	wāskahikan
47.	if	kīspin
48.	jump	kwāskohti
49.	man	nāpēw
50.	why	tānēhki
51.	many	mihcēt
52.	more	kīyāpic
53.	today	anohc

nēhiyawētān kīkināhk | *Speaking Cree in the Home*

54.	now	sēmāk
55.	only one	pēyak piko
56.	over	pāsci-
57.	put	astā
58.	some	ātiht
59.	think	māmitonēyīhta
60.	work	atoskē
61.	write	masināhikē
62.	stop	nakī
63.	people	ayisiyiniwak
64.	then	ispīhk
65.	see	wāpāhta (NI), wāpam (NA)
66.	come	āstam
67.	over there	nētē
68.	like (for instance)	tāpiskōc
69.	like (this)	ōmisi
70.	like (something)	miywēyihta
71.	old	kayāsi-
72.	once	pēyakwāw
73.	open	yōhtēna
74.	walk	pimohtē
75.	good	miywāsin
76.	new	oskāyi-
77.	no	namōya
78.	yes	āha, ahpō ēha

79.	soon	wīpac
80.	under	sīpā
81.	who	awīna
82.	put it away	nahastā
83.	throw it away	wēpina
84.	go away	awas
85.	don't	ēkāwiya
86.	girl	iskwēsis
87.	woman	iskwēw
88.	almost	kīkāc
89.	truly	tāpwē
90.	since	aspin
91.	where	tānitē
92.	where is	tāniwē (NI), tāniwā (NA)
93.	bring it, bring (NA)	pētā (NI), pēsiw (NA)
94.	well, please, let's see	mahti
95.	oh well, it's okay	kiyām
96.	be careful/carefully	papēyāhtak
97.	that's all/enough	ēkwāni
98.	me too	nīsta
99.	you too	kīsta
100.	him/her too	wīsta

CHAPTER TEN

isīhcikēwina kiya ēkwa kicawāsimis ohci

Activities for You and Your Child

Activity 1: Establishing Daily Routines in the Home

It is important for children to establish a morning and bedtime routine. It helps build a sense of security and stability when they know what to expect, but it will also help them develop good life habits. In addition, they will feel well rested.

The schedule was adapted from an English version and translated to Cree. To establish a repetitive series of words related to morning and bedtime is also good practice when working towards making Cree the language of your home.

You can create a chart and hang it up where it is visible, and you can make one with tabs or with checkmarks as each item is completed. It does not have to be in any particular order; you choose what works best for you.

waniskāwin / Time to Get Up		āsay (done) ✓
waniskā	(You) wake up	
postayiwinisē	(You) get dressed	
nāhastāsimonihkē ahpō anāskatiso	Make your bed	
kāsīhkwē	Wash your face	
kisīpēkāpitē	Brush your teeth	
sīkaho	Brush your hair	
mīciso	(You) eat	
postaskisinē ēkwa postasākē	Put your shoes and jacket on	
miyo-kīsikanisi	(You) have a good day	

isīhcikēwina kiya ēkwa kicawāsimis ohci | *Activities for You and Your Child*

kawisimo / Get Ready for Bed		āsay (done) ✓
nāhastāso	Put your stuff away	
kisīpēkinastē	(You) have a bath	
minihkwē nipiy	(You) drink water	
kisīpēkāpitē	Brush your teeth	
ayamihcikē	(You) read	
nēhiyawē	(You) speak Cree	
kākīsimo	(You) pray	
ākwaskitinikē ēkwa ocēmāwaso	(You give) hugs and kisses	
miyohkwāmi	(You) have a good sleep	

nēhiyawētān kīkināhk | *Speaking Cree in the Home*

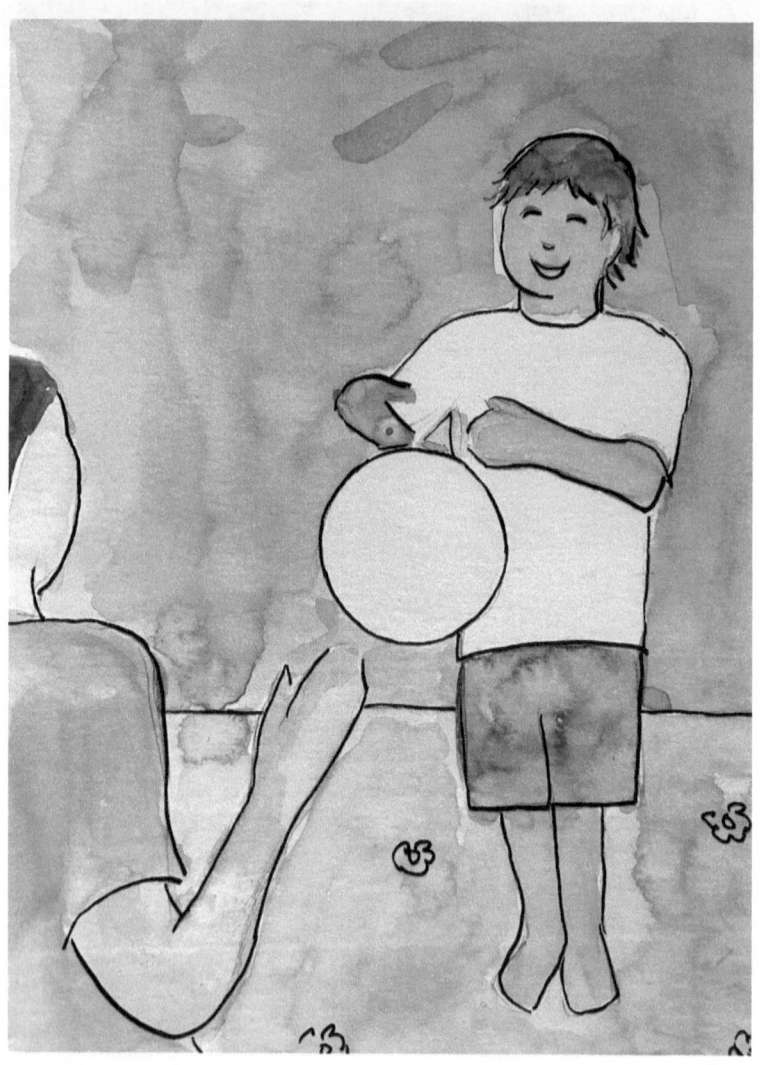

Activity 2: Conversational Cree

This game can be played anywhere with as many people as you would like. You can also use any type of question and response with this game. Make it even more fun by going faster as you begin to memorize the questions and how you respond to the questions.

MATERIALS:

- Ball (doesn't matter what size)
- Word list
- Two or more people

STEPS:

1. *Person 1*: Start with the question "tānisi?" and hold ball. Do not toss until *Person 2* responds.

2. *Person 2* responds with "namōya nānitaw." *Person 1* tosses the ball to *Person 2* after this response. *Person 2* catches the ball.

3. *Person 2* then faces *Person 3* and asks "tānisi?" and holds the ball until *Person 3* responds.

4. *Person 3* responds with "namōya nānitaw." *Person 2* then tosses the ball to *Person 3*.

5. Continue until all players have asked the question and answered the question.

Repeat with a different question:

1. *Person 1*: Start again with another question, "tānitē ohci kiya?" and hold the ball. Do not toss until *Person 2* responds.

2. *Person 2* responds with "_____ ohci niya." *Person 1* then tosses the ball to *Person 2*.

3. *Person 2* then faces *Person 3* and asks the same question to *Person 3*: "tānitē ohci kiya?"

4. *Person 3* then responds "_____ ohci niya." *Person 2* then tosses the ball to *Person 3*.

5. Continue going around until all players have asked and answered the question.

Other possible questions and responses

Question	Response
tānisi? (Hello, how are you?)	namōya nānitaw (I am fine.)
tānisi kitisiyihkāson? (What is your name?)	_____ nitisiyihkāson. (_____ is my name.)
tānitē ohci kiya? (Where are you from?)	_____ ohci niya (You can use English for place of residence if you don't have the Cree word)

isīhcikēwina kiya ēkwa kicawāsimis ohci | *Activities for You and Your Child*

tānitē kiwīkin mēkwāc? (Where are you currently living?)	_____ niwīkin mēkwāc. (You can use English for place of residence if you don't have the Cree word)
awīna kikāwiy? (Who is your mother?)	_____ nikāwiy. (_____ is my mother.)
awīna kohtāwiy? (Who is your father?)	_____ nohtāwiy. (_____ is my father.)
tānitē ē-itohtēyan? (Where are you going?)	_____ ē-itohtēyān. (I am going _____.) Note: it's not necessary to add "to the" in Cree like it is in English.
ki-nohtēhkatān cī? (Are you hungry?)	āha, ninohtēhkatān. (Yes, I am hungry.)
	namōya, namōya ninohtēhkatān. (No, I am not hungry.)
kinohtē-micison cī? (Do you want to eat?)	āha, asamin! (Yes, feed me!)
	namoya. (No.)
	namoya ninohtēkatān. (I am not hungry.)
tānisi ē-wī-itahkamikisiyan wāpahki? (What are you up to tomorrow?)	tānisi ētikwē. (I'm not sure.)
	niwī-nitawi-atoskān. (I am going to work.)
	There are many different response possibilities.

nēhiyawētān kīkinähk | Speaking Cree in the Home

Activity 3: Creating a Photo Album with Kinship Terms for Your Child

In Cree, the kinship system is quite complicated. There are terms that depend on whether you are female or male talking about a female or male relative. It is for this reason that only common relationship terms are used here.

MATERIALS:

- Cardstock paper
- Ribbon or yarn
- Printed images of your family
- Hole puncher
- Glue stick
- Marker or printed word list

STEPS:

1. Choose your layout (landscape or portrait) and size. Do you want them to be full-sized or half-sized?

2. Cut your cardstock paper accordingly, if you choose to make it half-sized.

3. The first page should be the person you are making it for.

4. Decide on the flow of your photo album. Who goes first, second, third, etc.

5. Match your vocabulary to that person. Use marker or print out your vocabulary word and glue it on.

6. Begin gluing your images to your cardstock and then add your vocabulary.

7. Finish the rest of your pages.

8. Decorate the photo album to your liking.

9. Punch holes where you want it to open from.

10. Put your ribbon through and tie it up.

11. Enjoy your new photo album!

12. Read repeatedly until you remember all the terms!

Vocabulary

wāhkōhtowin itwēwina / Kinship Terms: First Person Possessive	
Me, myself	niya
My name is _____	_____ nitisiyihkāson
This is my mom	nikāwiy awa

This is my dad	nohtāwiy awa
This is my older brother	nistēs awa
This is my older sister	nimis awa
This is my younger brother or sister (make as many as you need to)	nisīmis awa
This is my grandma	nōhkom awa
This is my grandpa	nimosōm awa
This is my uncle	nisis awa (My mother's brother) nōhkomis awa, ahpō nōhcāwīs awa (My father's brother, depending on region. Ask an Elder.)
This is my auntie	nisikos awa (My father's sister) nitōsis awa, ahpō nikāwīs awa (My mother's sister. Again, depends on region. Ask an Elder.)
This is my dog	nitīm awa
This is my cat	nipōsīsim awa, ahpō niminōsim awa (Ask for the word used in your area.)
Person who has passed on	add "**ipan**" to the end of the word to indicate your family or pets passing on (e.g., nohtāwīpan—my late father)

nēhiyawētān kīkināhk | *Speaking Cree in the Home*

Activity 4: Having a Meal with Your Family

MATERIALS:

- *Breakfast*:
  Bacon, eggs, toast, milk, water, juice, coffee, salt, pepper, cereal , oatmeal

- *Supper:*
  One of the following meat products: chicken, fish, beef
  One of the following sides: rice or potatoes
  One of the following vegetables: carrots or corn

STEPS:

1. Ask everyone to wash their hands.

2. Ask everyone to sit down around the table.

3. Say a prayer of thanks for the food.

4. Ask everyone to serve their own food.

5. For children: ask if they washed their hands.

Vocabulary

Wash your hands	kāsīcihcē (singular) kāsīcihcēk (plural)
Sit down (plural)	apik
Say prayer	kākīsimo
Make your plate/help yourself	kapatēhāmāso
Do you want some more:	kiyāpic cī kinōhtē–: (add the following)
Potatoes Rice Carrots Corn Chicken Meat Bacon Eggs Cereal	mīcin askipwāwa mōwāwak manōminak mōwāwak oskatākwak mōwāwak mahtāminak mōwāw pāhkahāhkwān mīcin wiyās mōwāw kohkōsiwiyin mīcin wāwa mīcin kīkisēpā-mīcowin
Taste it	kocispita (NI) kocispis (NA)
Bring the food	pētā anima mīciwin
Pass the pepper	pētā papīskomina

Pass the salt	pētā siwītakan
Feed yourself	asamiso
Wash the dishes	kāsīyākanē
Close your mouth	kipāha kitōn
Eat slowly	nanisīhkāc mīciso
Do you like the chicken?	kiwīhkipwāw cī pāhkahāhkwān?
Do you like the meat?	kiwīhkistēn cī wiyās?
Do you like the fish?	kiwīhkipwāw cī kinosēw?
Eat well	kwayask mīciso
This is good for you, it comes from the land	miywāsin ōma iyinato-mīciwin
Don't waste your food	ēkāwiya wiyakīhtā kimīciwin
This is not good for you—it might make you feel bad	ka-māyiskākon anima mīciwin
Your stomach might hurt: —There's too much salt —There's too much sugar —There's too much grease	ka-wīsakēyīhtēn katay (then add) osām mistahi sīwīhtākan osām mistahi sīwinikan osām mistahi pimiy

nēhiyawētān kīkināhk | *Speaking Cree in the Home*

Activity 5: Learning Body Parts with Your Child

MATERIALS: None required.

STEPS:

1. DAY ONE: Point at nose and say "nikot," then point to his/her nose and say "kikot."

2. DAY TWO: Repeat and add mouth. Point at mouth and say "nitōn," and then point to his/her mouth and say "kitōn."

3. Do these for a few days at first before you move on to other body parts: eye(s), ear(s), hair, hand(s), finger(s), leg(s), arm(s), stomach, shoulders, neck, chest, thigh, buttocks, foot, feet, toe(s).

4. Remember singular and plural forms for each of the terms.

5. EXTENSION: Play a game.
    a. "Where is your _____?" (Singular)
        i. For example: "Where is your nose? tāniwē kikot?"

    b. "Where are your _____?" (Plural)
        i. For example: "Where are your eyes? tāniwēhā kiskīsikwa?"

c. Each time he/she gets it correct, reward with praise. If he/she doesn't get it quite right say, "kīkāc—almost!" to encourage them and then say the correct term while pointing to the body part. Ask them to repeat after you.

d. Ask your child what patterns they are noticing if you want them to be aware of the differences between "my" and "your."
    i. "I/me" possessive markers usually start with "ni"; other variances include "no," "nō," and "na."

    ii. "You" possessive markers usually start with "ki"; other variances include "kī," "ko," and "ka."

Vocabulary

My face/Your face	nihkwākan/kihkwākan
My head/Your head	nistikwān/kistikwān
My hair/Your hair	nēstakaya/kēstakaya
My nose/Your nose	nikot/kikot
My mouth/Your mouth	nitōn/kitōn
My forehead/Your forehead	niskāhtik/kiskāhtik
My eye/Your eye My eyes/Your eyes	niskīsik/kiskīsik niskīsikwa/kiskīsikwa
My ear/ Your ear My ears/ Your ears	nīhtawakay/kīhtawakay nīhtawakaya/kīhtawakaya
My chin/ Your chin	nitāpiskan/kitāpiskan
My hand/ Your hand My hands/Your hands	nicihciy/kicihciy nicihciya/kicihciya
My finger/Your finger My fingers/Your fingers	niyīkicihcān/kiyīkicihcān niyīkicihcāna/kiyīkicihcāna
My arm/Your arm My arms/Your arms	nispiton/kispiton nispitona/kispitona

My stomach/Your stomach	natay/katay
My belly button/Your belly button My little belly button/Your little belly button	nitisiy/kitisiy nicisīs/kicisīs
My chest/Your chest	nāskikan/kāskikan
My shoulder/Your shoulder My shoulders/Your shoulders	nitihtiman/kitihtiman nitihtimana/kitihtimana
My neck/Your neck	nikwayaw/kikwayaw
My elbow/Your elbow My elbows/Your elbows	nitōskwan/kitōskwan nitōskwana/kitōskwana
My buttocks/Your buttocks	nisōkan/kisōkan
My thigh/Your thigh My thighs/Your thighs	nipwām/kipwām nipwāma/kipwāma
My knee/Your knee My knees/Your knees	nihcikwan/kihcikwan nihcikwana/kihcikwana
My foot/Your foot My feet/Your feet	nisit/kisit nisita/kisita
My toe/Your toe My toes/Your toes	niyiyīkisitān/kiyiyīkisitān niyiyīkisitāna/kiyiyīkisitāna

My nail/Your nail	naskasiy/kaskasiy
My nails/Your nails	naskasiyak/kaskasiyak
My _____ hurts.	niwīsakēyīhtēn _____
Insert body part on the blank line above.	
Does your _____ hurt?	kiwīsakēyīhtēn cī _____
Insert body part on the blank line above.	
I hurt my foot(feet).	niwīsakisitān
I hurt my head.	niwīsakistikwānān
I hurt my hand(s).	niwīsakicihcān
I hurt my nose.	niwīsakikotān
I hurt my leg(s).	niwīsakiskātān
I hurt my face.	niwīsakihkwākanān
My eyes hurt.	niwīsakēyihtēn niskīsikwa
My ears hurt.	niwīsakēyihtēn nīhtawakaya
I have a headache.	nitēyistikwānān
I have a fever./You have a fever.	nikisison/kikisison

nēhiyawētān kīkināhk | *Speaking Cree in the Home*

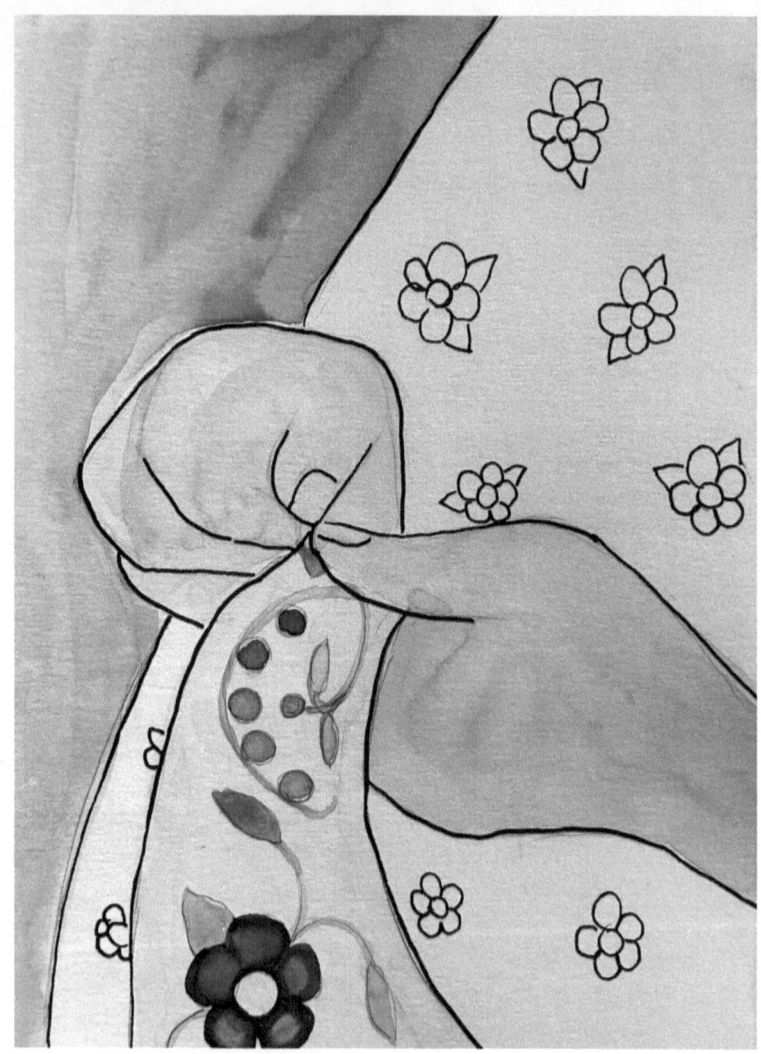

Activity 6: Beading

Beading is an ancient form of art. Traditionally, artisans would use natural materials that were available to them: materials such as stones, shells, bones, copper, and other natural materials. It is an art that demands hours of meticulous work that requires knowledge of art and design. Today many people do beadwork and it is a sign of resilience and pride in one's culture. Children learn first by observing and then by doing. Parents, grandparents, aunts, and uncles can pass on an ancient art while they teach patience and perseverance. The vocabulary list provided here is not meant to be comprehensive but is a list of words and phrases thought to be more common as one is beading.

MATERIALS:

- Beads
- Needles
- Scissors
- Thread
- Thimble
- Hide
- Pattern

STEPS:

1. One by one, show each item to your child and ask them to repeat in Cree after you.

2. Demonstrate each step slowly and say the words as you do them.

3. Offer praise and encourage them to keep trying.

4. Tell them to think good thoughts as they work: thinking bad thoughts could cause them to make mistakes or hurt themselves.

Vocabulary

Beads	mīkisak
Needle Needles	sāpōnikan sāpōnikana
Thread	asapāp
Hide	pāhkēkan
Bead (verb; as a command)	mīkisihkahcikē
Make moccasins	maskisinihkē
Pattern	masinisāwān
Draw	tapasinahikē
Scissors	paskwahamātowin
Thimble	kāskikwāsonāpisk
Draw the pattern on paper	tapasinaha masinisāwin tahkohc masinahikanihk
Put (the pattern) on your hide	tahkohc astā kipāhkēkanimihk
Put your thread on your needle	āhi asapāp sāponikanihk

Tie at the end	tahkopita kisipanohk
Pick up your beads with your needle	otinik kimīkisimak sāponikan ohci
Put your needle under your hide	sīpā ohci astā kisāponikan
Put your needle through your hide	sāpostaha pāhkēkin
Use two needles: one for the beads and one for tacking the beads down	nīso āpacihtā sāponikana: pēyak ohci mīkisak ēkwa pēyak ohci ta-sakāstahwacik mīkisak
Be patient	sīpēyihta
Careful	papēyāhtak
Cut the thread	kīskis ana asapāp
Where are the scissors?	tāniwē paskwahamātowin
Truly, it is beautiful!	tāpwē miyonākwan!
It is nice/good	miywāsin
Almost	kēkāc

NOTE: Beads in Cree are considered animate, so the colours used here describe animate objects.

Those red beads	kā-mihkosicik mīkisak
Those blue beads	kā-sīpihkosicik mīkisak
Those green beads	kā-askihtakosick mīkisak
Those white beads	kā-wāpiskisicik mīkisak
Those black beads	kā-kaskitēsicik mīkisak
Those yellow beads	kā-wāposāwisicik mīkisak
Those orange beads	kā-osāwisicik mīkisak
Those purple beads	kā-nīpāmāyātisicik mīkisak
Those pink beads	kā-wāpikwanīwicīkosicik mīkisak

nēhiyawētān kīkināhk | *Speaking Cree in the Home*

Activity 7: Berry Picking

MATERIALS:

- Pail

STEPS:

1. Find a pail or other container to put berries in.

2. Find bush.

3. Gather berries.

4. Do not pull from the roots.

5. Clean berries.

Vocabulary

Gather berries	mawiso
I am gathering berries	nimawison
She/he is gathering berries	mawisow
Eat berries as you pick them	mōminē
I am eating berries as I pick them	nimōminān

She/he is eating berries as she/he picks them	mōminēw
Little pail	askihkos
Container	asiwacikan
Little container	asiwacikanis
Raspberries (NA)	ayōskanak
Blueberries (NI)	iyinimina
Strawberries (NI)	otēhimina
Saskatoon berries (NI)	misāskatōmina
Chokecherries (NI)	takwahimināna
Cranberries (NI)	wīsakimina
Gooseberries (NI)	sāpōmina
Let's go pick berries	nitawi-mawisotān
Okay, I like picking berries	ahāw, nimiywēyihtēn ta-mawisoyān
I feel like going to pick berries	ninohtē-mawison
Let's pick a lot so we can use them for a long time	otinētān mistahi, kinwēsk ka-āpacihtāyāhk
Watch your step	itāpi ita kā-tahkoskēyan
Truly, you're good at picking berries	tāpwē kinihtā-mawison
I'm good at picking berries	ninihtā-mawison
You're fast at picking berries	tāpwē kikiyipān kā-mawisoyan
Don't go too far	ēkāwiya wāhyaw itohtē

Taste it (NI) Taste it (NA)	kocispita kocispis
Don't pull from the roots	ēkāwiya ocipita ocēpihkwa
Patience	sīpēyihta
Don't be in a rush	ēkāwiya papāsi

nēhiyawētān kīkināhk | *Speaking Cree in the Home*

Activity 8: Road Trip

After several road trips, the language used around road trips has become automatic. We get into the car, put our seatbelts on, and listen to music. Sometimes we pick up drinks for the trip.

MATERIALS: None required.

STEPS

1. Decide where you're going to just drive.
2. Decide if you're going to pick up drinks.
3. Choose a destination and ride!

Vocabulary

Car	sēhkēpayīs
Van	misiwētāpācīsk
Get into the car	pōsi-sēhkēpayīsihk
Jump in	pōsi-kwāskohti
Open the door	yōhtēna iskwāhtēm
Shut the door	kipāha iskwāhtēm

Put your seatbelt on	akwamohtā kipakwahtēhon
Play music	kitohcikē
This (song) sounds good	miyohtākwan
Turn the music up	kisīwēna
This (song) doesn't sound good	macihtākwan
Turn the music down	nīkina
Where do you want to go?	tānitē kinohtē-ispayin?
Do you want to stop?	kinohtē-kipihcān cī?
Yes, I want to stop here	āha, ninōhtē-kipihcān ōta
Do you want a (pop) drink?	kinōhtē-minihkwān cī sīwāpoy?
Yes, I want to get something (pop) to drink	āha, ninōhtē-minihkwān sīwāpoy
Do you want to go home?	kinōhtē-kīwān cī?
Can we go home now?	ka-kī-kīwānaw cī?
I don't want to go home yet	namōya cēskwa ninōhtē-kīwān

isīhcikēwina kiya ēkwa kicawāsimis ohci | *Activities for You and Your Child*

Activity 9: Nature Walk

MATERIALS:

- *nēhiyawēwin itwēwina*—Cree dictionary for words that are not listed here.

STEPS:

1. Get ready.

2. Walk.

3. Pay attention to the things you see and use the words you want to learn.

Vocabulary

Rock	asiniy
Rocks	asiniyak
Little rock	asinīsis
Little rocks	asinīsisak
Butterfly	kamāmak
Butterflies	kamāmakwak
Little butterfly	kamāmakos
Little butterflies	kamāmakosak
Bee	amō
Bees	amōwak

nēhiyawētān kīkināhk | *Speaking Cree in the Home*

isīhcikēwina kiya ēkwa kicawāsimis ohci | *Activities for You and Your Child*

Ant	ēyikos
Ants	ēyikosak
Ant hill	ēyikowīsti
Bird	piyēsīs
Birds	piyēsīsak
Bird's nest	piyēsīs waciston
Duck	sīsīp
Ducks	sīsīpak
Bug	manicōs
Bugs	manicōsak
Flower	wāpikwaniy
Flowers	wāpikwaniya
Soil	asiskiy
Sand	yēkaw
Trees	mistikwak
Cedar	māsikīsk
Birch tree	waskway
Red willow	mihwāpēmak
Willow	nīpisiy
White spruce tree	sihta
Black spruce tree	minahik
Poplar tree	mītos
Black poplar	māyi-mītos
Jack pine	oskāhtak

nēhiyawētān kīkinähk | *Speaking Cree in the Home*

Forest	sakāw
Sun	pīsim
Wind	yōtin
Rain	kimiwan
Drizzle	kimiwasin
Cloud Clouds	waskow waskoya
It is cloudy	yīkiskwan
It is a warm day	kīsōwayāw
It is a very warm day	kīsopwēw
It is a very hot day	kisāstēw
It is a chilly day	cahkāyāsin
It is a cold day	tahkāyāw
It is a very cold day	kisināāw
It is a beautiful day	miyo-kīsikāw
It is a bad day (weather)	maci-kīsikāw
It is a cold wind	tahkiyowēw
Lake	sākahikan
River	sipiy
Pond	sākahikanisis
Put your clothing on	postayiwinisē

isīhcikēwina kiya ēkwa kicawāsimis ohci | *Activities for You and Your Child*

Put your shoes on	postaskisinē
Put your jacket on	postasākē
Put your hat on	postastotinē
Put your mitts on	postastisē
Take your clothing off	kētayiwinisē
Take your shoes off	kētaskisinē
Take your jacket off	kētasākē
Take your hat off	kētastotinē
Take your mitts off	kētastisē
Take some tobacco	tahkon cistēmāw
Don't go far	ēkāwiya wāhyaw itohtē
This is medicine	maskihkiy ōma
Walk slowly so you can look around	papēyāhtak pimohtē ta-papāmi-itāpēyan
The land looks beautiful	takahkinākwan askiy
Be thankful for everything	nanāskomo kahkiyaw kīkway ohci

nēhiyawētān kīkināhk | *Speaking Cree in the Home*

Activity 10: Smudge and Prayer

We debated on whether to include a section on smudging and praying. Ultimately, we decided that it is important to include this as a tool for reclaiming traditional practices, which include spirituality. We strongly believe that children need to be taught about faith and a higher power whom we know as kisē-manitow—kind, compassionate, and loving Creator—so that in times of hardship, they will always know that they are protected and loved. They should also be taught to be careful about what they pray for; they should keep prayers short and be mindful of what they are praying for.

NOTE: These are only suggestions and how we teach our children. Remember that there is no one way to pray and we must respect each other and all the different ways we pray.

MATERIALS:

- Sage
- Matches
- Prayer
- Smudge bowl

Steps:

1. Create an area where you go to say your prayers and smudge.

2. You can smudge in the morning and at night. When and how often is at your discretion.

3. Demonstrate with your child and say each term one at a time. Ask them to repeat after you.

4. Try to use the same words until they become automatic. This may take a long time and that is okay.

Vocabulary

Sage	paskwāwihkwask
Smudge (with sweetgrass)	miyāhkasikē
I smudge my eyes to see good things	nimiyāhkasēn niskīskwa ta-wāhpatamān ē-miywāsik kīkway
I smudge my ears to hear good things	nimiyāhkasēn nīhtawakaya ta-pēhtamān miyo-kīkwaya
I smudge my mouth to say good things	nimiyāhkasēn nitōn kwayask ta-miyo-pīskwēyān
I smudge my head to think good thoughts	nimiyāhkasēn nistikwān kwayask ta-mamitonēyihtamān
I smudge my heart so I can be kind	nimiyāhkasēn niteh ta-kisēwātisiyān
I smudge my stomach so I can have courage	nimiyāhkasēn natay ta-sōhkitēhēyān
Thank you	ay hay kinanāskomitin

isīhcikēwina kiya ēkwa kicawāsimis ohci | *Activities for You and Your Child*

kākīsimowin / Prayer	
Pray	kākīsimo
Kind, compassionate, and loving Creator	kisē-manitow
We are grateful for all your gifts	kinanāskomitinān kahkiyaw ohci kīkway kā-miyiyāhk
Help us and protect us	wīcihinān mīna sawēyiminān
Your children	niyanān kitawāsimisak
This night	anohc kā-tipiskāk
Help us to speak Cree and to be Cree	wīcihinān ta-nēhiyawēyāhk ēkwata-nēhiyawātisiyāhk
Protect all people and my family	sawēyimik kahkiyaw ayisiyiniwak ēkwa niwāhkōmākanak
Thank you, we are grateful	hay hay kitatamihinān

CHAPTER ELEVEN

sīhkimitowina

Inspirational Quotes

It is important to note, the following quotes were useful in our journeys of language reclamation and language teaching in education; these quotes came from a variety of other language warriors during conversations and/or attending language conferences (or are sometimes our own). We are grateful to 'echo' their sentiments.

- To speak Cree is to heal yourself, your family, and your community, it is practicing well-being.

- Learning a language is hard, but what a journey it will be in bringing Cree home.

- Language revitalization is a process. Setting up an environment is very much like moving into a new home.

- It is our role and responsibility to help children choose to be speakers.

- Learning a second or even a third language is beneficial for the speaker in multiple ways: problem solving, music, and math will come much easier, and it will open new worl dviews.

- Mistakes are good when learning a language. They help us figure out what a speaker needs to know by and through experience.

- nēhiyaw māmitonēyihta—Think in Cree.

- The brain must be in the language.

- Never translate!

- Be in the context and speak the language, show, demonstrate, get your point across! This is cognition.

- Reading in the brain is different than speaking in the brain. There is no articulation of sounds.

- Listen first and then speak second.
- Teach to think in the language.
- People want to learn the language. Role model it.
- Language reclamation is pieces of cultural history made present.
- Language revitalization is always in process.
- Success does not necessarily mean increasing the number of fluent speakers but engaging those that want to be learners/speakers.
- When teaching a language, personality is helpful.
- Fluency is not the only focus and demanding it could be harmful.
- Learners need to be trained to learn.
- Teach how you learn, not how you were taught.
- Remember that new speakers, they decide to be one for several positive reasons. Continue to be encouraging.

- Instil an intrinsic motivation to learn the language by being around other speakers.

- The Cree language is alive, it is spiritual, it is a part of you.

- nēhiyawēwin has power!

- Learning nēhiyawēwin is a sacred act.

- Learning nēhiyawēwin is resistance to assimilation

- Language reclamation is 'falling in love" with our people.

- Do not fixate on pronunciation.

- To speak nēhiyawēwin is to expose yourself: it is like rebuilding as a nation.

- Place names in Cree teach you how to respect the land.

- nēhiyawēwin is intimately tied to responsibilities.

- Once you know a word in Cree, make it a point to never use that word in English again.

- If you fail to practice today, wake up the next day and try again.

- ēkāwiya wīhkāc pakicī—never give up.

- Talk to others in Cree, have discussions with them about teaching Cree in the home. Inspire others to walk with you in your language reclamation journey.

- Celebrate any and all victories: when you learn a word, when you remember a word, when you stay in the language for a period of time, for visiting and speaking Cree, for making the effort, etc., it's all worth celebrating!

- Learning nēhiyawēwin is a lifelong journey

- Visit Elders and elderly relatives who speak the language—they need you and you need them.

- Have fun with your child; they must know that it can be fun to learn the language.

- nēhiyawēwin needs you!

- The plants, trees, rocks, and lakes miss their nēhiyawēwin names.

nanāskomowin

Acknowledgements

I am grateful to the nēhiyaw Language Spirit for choosing me to be a part of this life-saving work that has been my livelihood and my way home, 'nēhiyawak ōma kiyānaw' ēkwa nēhiyaw ōma niya. I am indebted to the language warriors who were trailblazing well ahead of me. hay hay to the late Dr. Freda Ahenakew and the (old) Saskatchewan Cree Language Retention Committee.

I would also like to acknowledge my grandparents, (late) Vital and (late) Mary Daniels, my father, aunts, and uncles of Sturgeon Lake First Nation, Saskatchewan, for speaking our language and continuing to speak Cree. I thank my children and grandchild (and those yet to come), who made me think deeply about language, land, identity, and their inheritance. I thank my husband, Quin, who has been supportive of my language work and encouraged me at every turn, bump, and paved route. I thank my nēhiyawak-speaking community, who have become my extended family, known as the nēhiyawak Language Experience, and friends in second-language acquisition, applied linguistics, and language revitalization. kinanāskomitināwāw mistahi!

—Belinda Daniels

First and foremost, I would like to acknowledge my mother, my late father, and my late grandparents Andrew and Sophie Custer and Maggie and William Highway. I would also like to acknowledge numerous aunts, uncles, cousins, and my home community for giving me the invaluable gift of the nīhithaw language and always keeping me grounded in who I am and where I come from. I am forever grateful for your gifts. I would also like to thank my children, who have inspired my work in language revitalization; Jean Okimāsis and Arok Wolvengrey for their help in translating some of the more challenging and newer vocabularies; Solomon Ratt for editing the SRO; and Anne Clarke, my dear chākos, who is also a Cree linguist and teacher with whom I have numerous conversations about our language—she has also helped me translate and edit some vocabulary in this manual; my husband, Randy Clarke, who teaches Scarlett and Andrew about our traditional harvesting practices and supports me in our everyday efforts to stay in the language at home. Lastly, I'd like to thank all the trailblazers who paved the way for us to do this kind of work. Thank you for never giving up on the language and your tireless work in revitalizing the language.

kinanāskomitināwāw kahkithaw—I am grateful to you all.

—Andrea Custer

Notes

1. The following three indented quotes are from Ella Elizabeth Clark, *Indian Legends of Canada* (United States: McClelland & Stewart, 2011), 7–9.
2. W.A. Waiser, *A World We Have Lost: Saskatchewan Before 1905* (Markham: Fifth House, 2016).
3. Quoted in Waiser, 54.
4. Truth and Reconciliation Commission of Canada, *Honouring the Truth, Reconciling for the Future: Summary of the Final Report of the Truth and Reconciliation Commission of Canada* (Ottawa, 2015), 51.
5. D. Jung, M. Klein, and S. Stoll, "Language Transition(s): School Responses to Recent Changes in Language Choice in a Northern Dene Community (Canada), in *Language Practices of Indigenous Children and Youth*, eds G. Wigglesworth, J. Simpson, and J. Vaughan (London: Palgrave Macmillan, 2018), 54.
6. Jung, Klein, and Stoll, "Language Transition(s)," 56.
7. We are to abide by Natural laws, and there are many. One of these is that family and children are sacred.
8. We are to use our mouths wisely because our words have power, i.e., we are not to hurt the spirit of others by gossiping or putting them down.
9. We are not to torture or disrespect animals.
10. Don't ever be afraid of anything.
11. othāpahcikīw is an ancestor of mine on both my maternal and paternal side from the 1800s who is said to have had supernatural powers; he had the ability to see into the future, fought with wīhtikow, and practiced vision quests.
12. Leading a good life; someone who lives by the Natural laws, values and teachings of their community.

13 The child did not cry a lot because he/she was born loved.
14 The child would not be hyper and out of control.
15 You have caused them to disobey the Natural laws, which has consequences.
16 We are the (Plains) Cree people.
17 Leanne Hinton (ed.), *Bringing Our Languages Home: Language Revitalization for Families* (Berkeley, CA: Heyday Books, 2013).
18 S. Krashen and T. Terrell, *The Natural Approach: Language Acquisition in the Classroom* (London: Prentice Hall, 1998), 18; emphasis added.
19 W. Ermine, "Pedagogy from the Ethos: An Interview with Elder Ermine on Language," in *As We See . . . Aboriginal Pedagogy*, ed. Lenore A. Stiffarm (Saskatoon: University Extension Press, 1993), 18.
20 You can find Brian MacDonald's CD, *Cree Songbook*, at Saskatchewan Indigenous Cultural Centre (SICC) in Saskatoon. Darlene Auger's CD is available through her website "wîwîp'son" (http://wiwipson.com/cd-of-cree-lullabies/). It is also available through Spotify, Apple Music, and Amazon.
21 You can purchase Eaglecrest's Cree/nēhiyaw Standard Roman Orthography books online at https://eaglecrestbooks.com/order-books-english-cree.html; Celia Deschambault's book is available here: jerbearbooks.ca; and Arok Wolvengrey's dictionaries are available at the McNally Robinson bookstore in Saskatoon or can be ordered online at www.mcnallyrobinson.com.
22 mbcradio.com offers Cree programming online throughout the week at different times. See the website for more information. You will find more information on MBC's Cree programming by selecting Languages from the About Us menu.
23 For examples of the sound system see the following links: https://creeliteracy.org/beginning-to-read-plains-cree-in-standard-roman-orthography/sounds-of-sro/ and https://www.learncreewithandrea.com/post/cree-sound-system.

References

Basso, K. *Wisdom Sits in Places: Landscapes and Language among the Western Apache*. Albuquerque: University of New Mexico Press, 1996.

Battiste, M. *Decolonization Education*. Saskatoon: Purich Publishing, 2013.

Battiste, M. (ed). *Reclaiming Indigenous Voice and Vision*. Vancouver: University of British Columbia Press, 2000.

Blair, H., and Freedeen, S. "Putting Knowledge into Practice." *Canadian Journal of Native Education* 32, no. 2 (2009): 62–77.

Blair, H., Rice, S., Wood, V., and Janvier, J. "Daghida: Cold Lake First Nations Works towards Dene Language Revitalization." In Burnaby and Reyhner, *Indigenous Languages across the Community*, 89–98.

Burnaby, B. "Aboriginal Language Maintenance Development and Enhancement." In *Stabilizing Indigenous Languages*, edited by G. Cantoni, 21–36. Rev. ed. Flagstaff: Northern Arizona University Press, 2007.

Burnaby, B., and Reyhner, J. A. (eds). *Indigenous Languages across the Community*. Flagstaff: Northern Arizona University, 2002.

Cajete, G. *Native Science*. Santa Fe: Clear Light Publishers, 2000.

Cajete, G. "Indigenous Knowledge: The Pueblo Metaphor of Indigenous Education." In *Reclaiming Indigenous Voice and Vision*, edited by M. Battiste, 181–91. Vancouver: University of British Columbia Press, 2000.

Clark, E. E. *Indian Legends of Canada*. Toronto: McClelland & Stewart, 1960.

Cruikshank, J. *Life Lived like a Story*. Nebraska: University of Nebraska, 1990.

Custer, A. "Cree Sound System." Learn Cree With Andrea & Family. Last modified April 14, 2019. https://www.learncreewithandrea.com/post/cree-sound-system.

Daniels-Fiss, B. "My Journey of Learning the Cree Language." MA thesis, University of Saskatchewan, Department of Educational Foundations, 2009.

Daniels, B. C. "A Whisper of True Learning." *LEARNing Landscapes* 7, no. 2 (2014): 101–14. https://doi.org/10.36510/learnland.v7i2.653.

Daschuk, J. *Clearing The Plains: Disease, Politics of Starvation, and the Loss of Indigenous Life*. Regina: University of Regina Press, 2019.

Dickason, O., and Newbigging, W. *Indigenous Peoples within Canada: A Concise History*. 4th ed. Don Mills, ON: Oxford University Press, 2018.

Ermine, W. "Pedagogy from the Ethos: An Interview with Elder Ermine on Language." In *As We See . . . Aboriginal Pedagogy*, edited by Lenore A. Stiffarm, 9–28. Saskatoon: University Extension Press, 1993.

Fixico, D. *The American Indian Mind in a Linear World*. New York: Routledge, 2014.

Funk, J., and Lobe, G. "Passes and Permits." In *And They Told Us Their Stories*, edited by F. Funk, 23–8. Saskatoon: Saskatoon District Tribal Council, 1991.

Graveline, F. J. *Circleworks: Transforming Eurocentric Consciousness*. Halifax: Fernwood Publishing, 1998.

Hinton, L. (ed). *Bringing Our Languages Home: Language Revitalization for Families.* Berkeley, CA: Heyday Books, 2013.

Hinton, L., and Hale, K. *The Green Book of Language Revitalization in Practice*. San Diego: Academic Press, 2001.

"History of Residential Schools." Indigenous Peoples Atlas of Canada. Accessed March 24, 2022. https://indigenouspeoplesatlasofcanada.ca/article/history-of-residential-schools/.

Jung, D., Klein, M., and Stoll, S. "Language Transition(s): School Responses to Recent Changes in Language Choice in a Northern Dene Community (Canada)." In *Language Practices of Indigenous Children and Youth: The Transition from Home to School*, edited by G. Wigglesworth, J. Simpson, and J. Vaughan. London: Palgrave Macmillan, 2018. https://doi.org/10.1057/978-1-137-60120-9_3.

King, J. "Te Kohanga Reo: Maori Language Revitalization." In Hinton and Hale, *The Green Book of Language Revitalization in Practice*, 119–28.

Kirkness, V. "The Preservation and Use of Our Languages: Respecting the Natural Order of the Creator." In Burnaby and Reyhner, *Indigenous Languages across the Community*, 17–23.

Krashen, S., and Terrell, T. *The Natural Approach: Language Acquisition in the Classroom*. London: Prentice Hall, 1998.

Littlebear, L. YouTube video. https://www.youtube.com/watch?v=ycQtQZ9y3l.

McIvor, O. "Strategies for Indigenous Language Revitalization and Maintenance." In *Encyclopaedia of Language and Literacy Development*, 1–12. London, ON: Canadian Language and Literary Research Network, 2009.

McIvor, O., and Anisman, A. "Keeping Our Languages Alive: Strategies for Indigenous Language Revitalization and Maintenance." In *Handbook of Cultural Security*, edited by Yasushi Watanabe, 90–109. Cheltenham: Edward Elgar Publishing, 2018. https://www.elgaronline.com/view/edcoll/9781786437730/9781786437730.00011.xml.

McLeod, N. *Cree Narrative Memory: From Treaties to Contemporary Times*. Saskatoon: Purich Publishing, 2007.

Millar, J. R. *Shingwauk's Vision: A History of Native Residential Schools*. Toronto: University of Toronto Press, 1996.

"nehiyaw masinahikan." Online Cree Dictionary. Accessed March 24, 2022. creedictionary.com.

Okimāsis, J. *Cree: Language of the Plains*. Regina: Canadian Plains Research Center, 2004.

Ratt, S. Audio files. In A. Ogg, "Sounds of SRO," Cree Literacy Network, January 26, 2016. https://creeliteracy.org/beginning-to-read-plains-cree-in-standard-roman-orthography/sounds-of-sro/.

Sterzuk, A. "Building Language Teacher Awareness of Colonial Histories and Imperialistic Oppression through the Linguistic Landscape." In *Language Teaching in the Linguistic Landscape: Mobilizing Pedagogy in Public Space*, edited by S. Dubreil, D. Malinowski, and H. Maxim. Cham: Springer Nature, 2020.

Truth and Reconciliation Commission of Canada. *Honouring the Truth, Reconciling for the Future: Summary of the Final Report of the Truth and Reconciliation Commission of Canada*. Ottawa, 2015.

Tuck, E., McKenzie, M., and McCoy, K. "Land Education: Indigenous, Post-colonial, and Decolonizing Perspectives on Place and Environmental Education Research." *Environmental Education Research* 20, no. 1 (2014): 1–23. DOI: 10.1080/13504622.2013.877708.

Warner, S. N. "The Movement to Revitalize Hawaiian Language and Culture." In Hinton and Hale, *The Green Book of Language Revitalization in Practice*, 133–46.

Waiser, B. *A World We Have Lost: Saskatchewan before 1905*. Markham: Fifth House, 2016.

Wilson, A., Custer, A., and Daniels, B. "Indigenous Language Recovery: Land, Cultural Identity, and Education." Unpublished research paper, Aboriginal Research Education Centre, University of Saskatchewan, Saskatoon, 2017.

Wolvengrey, A. *nehiyawewin: itwewina. Cree: Words*. 2 vols. Regina: Canadian Plains Research Center, 2002.

Belinda (kakiyosēw) Daniels, PhD

Belinda niya, māka kakiyosēw ninēhiyaw-isiyihkāson. pakitawākan sākihkan ohci niya, Saskatchewanihk. māka Victoria, BC, mēkwāc niwīkin. okiskinwāhamākēw niya, nitatoskawāwak University of Victoria ēkwa nēhiyawak Language Experience Inc. niya ōma ē-kakwē-kiskinwāhamākosiyān nēhiyawēwin. ēkosi.

Belinda Daniels is the mother of four children and a grandmother to one, married, and resides in Victoria, BC. She is the founder of nēhiyawak Language Experience Inc. (2003), a not-for-profit language revitalization organization. Belinda was raised by her maternal grandparents in her home community of Sturgeon Lake, Saskatchewan. Later in life, after undergraduate studies, she began a journey in language recovery, is self-taught, and now teaches others about language reclamation work. Belinda is currently an assistant professor at the University of Victoria, BC, in Indigenous Education. Belinda has been recognized by the Canadian Teachers Federation and received the Outstanding Aboriginal Educator Award in 2015, along with the University of Saskatchewan Graduate Research Award in 2015. She was recognized globally as one of the top fifty finalists for the Global Teacher Prize in 2016. She not only teaches but also writes curriculum—her last project was with the National Collaborating Center on Indigenous Education. Belinda volunteers and sits on several boards, including the Foundation for Endangered Languages (Canada), where she was a past president and now a member at large. Belinda consistently demonstrates a commitment to language revitalization and land-based learning.

Photo by Tenille Campbell, Sweetmoon Photography.

Andrea Sherry Custer, BA, BEd, MEd

mihko-asiniy-iskwīw nitisithihkāson, māhtāwi-sīpihk ohci. tāpiskōc nōhkomak, nimosōmak ikwa nitāniskocāpānak kayās ohci omīthow askiy kā-pī-wīkicik, ī-pimātisihisocik ikwa ī-maskawātisicik. *My Cree name is Red Rock Woman, originally from* māhtāwi sīpiy *like my grandmothers, grandfathers, and great-grandparents before me; they have lived there, thrived there, and have gotten their strength from those territories since time immemorial.*

Her English name is Andrea Custer and she is a mother of five children. She is Woodland Cree and a fluent Cree speaker who grew up in wapāwikoscikanihk (*Narrows of Fear*), also known as Pelican Narrows. She has roots on the Churchill and Sturgeon Weir River systems in northern Saskatchewan, coming from a long line of traditional harvesters and land users in the iskwatam and askihk Lake areas. Andrea has a BA degree in Indigenous Studies from First Nations University, a secondary-level BEd teaching degree from the University of Alberta, and an MEd from the University of Saskatchewan in Indigenous Land-Based Education. Andrea currently works at First Nations University as a Cree language lecturer. Prior to this position she worked in Sturgeon Lake as the elementary Cree teacher, at Saskatchewan Indigenous Cultural Centre as the Cree language developer, and she has taught in Beauval, Saskatchewan, and in Maskwacis, Alberta, as a junior-high Cree language teacher. Her passion is in the area of language revitalization. Andrea is inspired by the love she holds for her children, family, mentors, home community, ancestors, and powerful history. Working with language has helped her understand that language teaches us about who we are, where we come from, and where we need to go. She understands that language shapes our beliefs and values, which in turn affect our attitudes and behaviours. There is an intricate connection.

Photo by H.B. Photography.

Other Cree Language Resources
Available from University of Regina Press

Visit www.uofrpress.ca for more information on these and other URP books.

nēhiyawēwin: itwēwina /
Cree: Words
compiled by Arok Wolvengrey
2 volume dictionary: English to
Cree; Cree to English
PB 9780889771277

mâci-nêhiyawêwin /
Beginning Cree
by Solomon Ratt,
illustrated by Holly Martin
COIL-BOUND 9780889774353

âhkami-nêhiyawêtân /
Let's Keep Speaking Cree
by Solomon Ratt
COIL-BOUND 9780889778467

kayās nōhcīn / I Come
from a Long Time Back
by Mary Louise
Rockthunder, wêpanâkit
PB 978088977838

nēhiyawēwin:
paskwāwi-pīkiskwēwin /
Cree: Language of the Plains
NEW EDITION
by Jean L. Okimāsis
PB 9780889777675

nēhiyawēwin:
paskwāwi-pīkiskwēwin /
Cree: Language of the Plains
LANGUAGE LAB WORKBOOK
by Jean L. Okimāsis
PB 9780889778856

nēhithaw ācimowina /
Woods Cree Stories
by Solomon Ratt
PB 9780889773455

wawiyatācimowinisa /
Funny Little Stories
edited by Arok Wolvengrey
PB 9780889771857

www.ingramcontent.com/pod-product-compliance
Lightning Source LLC
Chambersburg PA
CBHW032038290426
44110CB00012B/849